BEDLAM

Nell Leyshon

BEDLAM

OBERON BOOKS
LONDON

First published in 2010 by Oberon Books Ltd
521 Caledonian Road, London N7 9RH
Tel: 020 7607 3637 / Fax: 020 7607 3629
e-mail: info@oberonbooks.com
www.oberonbooks.com

Reprinted in 2011

A catalogue record for this book is available from the British
Library.

ISBN: 978-1-84943-052-4

Cover illustration by Adam Hayes

Printed in Great Britain by CPI Antony Rowe, Chippenham.

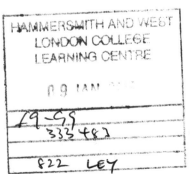

Acknowledgements:

Many thanks to: Bethlem Royal Hospital Archives and Museum Service, Dr Tim McInerny and his patients and staff at Bethlem and The Library of The English Folk Dance and Song Society.

BEDLAM

First perfomed at Shakespeare's Globe Theatre, London
on the 5th September 2010 with the following cast

Cast

DR CAREW, Jason Baughan
JOHN, Patrick Brennan
BILLY, Daon Broni
DR MAYNARD, Phil Cheadle
LAURENCE, Sam Crane
SAL, Sophie Duval
SAMUEL, Kevork Malikyan
RICHARD, Sean Kearns
TOM O'BEDLAM, James Lailey
OLIVER, Danny Lee Wynter
MAY, Rose Leslie
ANNABEL, Barbara Marten
MATTHEW, Joseph Timms
PHYLLIS, Ella Smith
STELLA, Lorna Stuart
GARDENIA, Finty Williams
NANCY, Jade Williams

BEDLAMITES
Charlotte Dodds, Alex Shaw, Jessica White, Chris Wynn

MUSICIANS
Mark Bousie, Andy Robinson, Corrina Silvester

Creative Team
Written by Nell Leyshon
Directed by Jessica Swale
Designed by Soutra Gilmour
Composed by Olly Fox

Characters

Act One

It is the eighteenth century and London is a brutal city of noise, stench and chaos. Streets are full of gin sellers, drunkards and animals.

The BEDLAMITES, a troupe of ex-inmates of Bedlam, specially licensed to play music, enter.

Others enter through the audience, picking fights and pockets on their way. They all gather on the street and join in the song.

To find my Tom of Bedlam, ten thousand miles I'd travel,
Mad Maudlin goes with dirty toes, to save her shoes from gravel.

Yet still I sing bonny boys, bonny mad boys, The Bedlam boys are bonny
They all go bare and they live by the air and they want no drink or money.

I went down to Satan's kitchen, for to buy some food one morning,
And there I got souls piping hot, which on the spit were turning.

Yet still I sing bonny boys, bonny mad boys, The Bedlam boys are bonny
They all go bare and they live by the air and they want no drink or money.

I now repent that ever, poor Tom was so disclaimed,
My wits I've lost since him I crossed which makes thus go chained.

Yet still I sing bonny boys, bonny mad boys, The Bedlam boys are bonny
They all go bare and they live by the air and they want no drink or money.

My staff hath murdered giants, my bag a long knife carries,
To cut mince pies from children's thighs with which to feast
the fairies.

Yet still I sing bonny boys, bonny mad boys, The Bedlam
boys are bonny
They all go bare and they live by the air and they want no
drink or money.

No gypsy, slut or doxie shall steal my Mad Tom from me,
I'll weep all night and with stars fight, the fray will well
become me.

Yet still I sing bonny boys, bonny mad boys, The Bedlam
boys are bonny
They all go bare and they live by the air and they want no
drink or money.

A spirit as hot as lightning, did on my travels guide me,
The sun did shake and pale moon quake whenever that
they spied me.

Yet still I sing bonny boys, bonny mad boys, The Bedlam
boys are bonny
They all go bare and they live by the air and they want no
drink or money.

And when that I have beaten the man in the moon to
powder,
His dog I'll take and him I'll make howl as no demon
louder.

Yet still I sing bonny boys, bonny mad boys, The Bedlam
boys are bonny
They all go bare and they live by the air and they want no
drink or money.

To find my Tom of Bedlam, ten thousand miles I'd travel,
Mad Maudlin goes with dirty toes, to save her shoes from
gravel.

Yet still I sing bonny boys, bonny mad boys, The Bedlam
boys are bonny
They all go bare and they live by the air and they want no
drink or money.

*A gin seller, PHYLLIS, enters with her barrow and cups and the crowd
rushes forward and queues for gin. The NARRATOR helps her.*

PHYLLIS: Gin. Get your gin.
Kill-grief. Heart's ease. Kick in the guts. Strip me naked.
Drunk for one penny.
Dead drunk for two penny.
Clean straw for nothing.

A BEGGAR calls out,

BEGGAR: Gis a penny. Only a penny.

and is chased away by the NARRATOR.

PHYLLIS hands gin out to a WOMAN.

PHYLLIS: Get your Lady's Delight.

PHYLLIS grabs a MAN.

Sir. Come and have a taste of heaven. Sip the nectar of
youth and eternal joy.

*The MAN pushes PHYLLIS away and she falls. Another MAN comes
to her help and a fight breaks out between the two men. As they
fight, the crowd circles and starts betting as the fight transforms into
a bare knuckle contest.*

BOOKIE: Put your money on now. Blood or no returns. Odds
on he'll knock him sky high.
Put your money on now.
Pennies to pounds.
That's it. Stand back. Watch for the blood.

MAN: Hit him.

WOMAN: Get him.

MAN: Upper cut.

WOMAN: Kill him.

As the fight progresses, two cockerels are released from baskets, and the fight transforms into a cock fight, the cocks blinkered with metal spurs on their heels.

BOOKIE: Cock to win.
Pennies to pounds.

MAN: Get him.

WOMAN: Kill him.

MAN: I'll kill you.

A sedan chair is carried on. The fight breaks up as everyone surrounds the sedan.

A finely dressed man, LAURENCE, steps out.

The gin seller calls out.

PHYLLIS: Get your gin.
Gin.

A PROSTITUTE parades, watched by all, then stops centre stage and lifts her skirts in front of LAURENCE.

PROSTITUTE: You look like a gentle man, sir.
Give a girl a bob. Cross her palm and she'll show you the way to heaven.
She'll give God a run for his money.

She circles him.

Let me rid you of your load, sir. It's a lot to carry.
Here.

She shows him under her skirt.

Come on, sir. I'm a clean girl. You could stick your head under there and you'd come up smelling of roses.

LAURENCE laughs and picks his way through the crowd. PHYLLIS hands the PROSTITUTE some gin. The crowd circle her and cheer as she downs the glass in one then falls to the ground.

The rough music begins: banging and crashing of plates, pots, pans and marrow bones. A cacophony of noise and shouting:

CROWD: Hedge whore. Hedge whore.
Hedge whore. Hedge whore.

The NARRATOR steps forward.

NARRATOR: Enough. Enough.

The music stops.

Get out. Go on. Out.

The crowd disperses.

I am a Bedlamite. Thrown out the asylum, into the streets to sing for pennies. Tom o'Bedlam, that's me.

He begs from the audience.

So I ask you to empty out your pockets. Have a bit of compassion. You got to sing for your supper, you got to sing for your drink, you got to sing for your pillow. Come on, let the moths fly free from your purse. You don't look short of a bob, sir. Thank you.

Thank you, sir. Thank you.

The NARRATOR and the BEDLAMITES sing as they leave.

SONG: To find my Tom of Bedlam, ten thousand miles I'd travel,
Mad Maudlin goes with dirty toes, to save her shoes from gravel.

Yet still I sing bonny boys, bonny mad boys, The Bedlam boys are bonny
They all go bare and they live by the air and they want no drink or money.

SCENE ONE

The asylum. It is a Saturday, the day of discharges and admissions.

DR SIDNEY CAREW strides into the room. He is finely dressed, wears a silk top hat. He is restless, energetic. MATTHEW, his clumsy and thickset son, follows carrying some paperwork, dropping it and tripping over. CAREW watches, impatient.

DR CAREW: Stand up, son. Walk straight. Watch it. Oh, for God's sake. Pick it up. Pick it up.

SAMUEL enters from opposite and sets himself up to act as scribe, opens books. CAREW hurries him.

Come on, man. We need them in and out. No time for hesitation, niceties, formalities.

SAMUEL: I'm ready, sir.

DR CAREW: Praise the Lord. Who do we have?

SAMUEL: John James.

A MAN is dragged forward by SAL, the gallery maid.

DR CAREW: Observe, Matthew, how the mouth hangs open. A slow brain and doubtful moral fibre. What was his case?

MATTHEW: Lovesickness? Religious excess?

DR CAREW: He is boanthropic.

MATTHEW: What is boba-bobanthrobic?

DR CAREW: What have you between the lug holes? Give it a shake. Recall, son. Recall? Bo – bovine. Anthropoid – man-like.
James. Do you still believe you are a cow?

MAN: I am a man, sir.

DR CAREW: Good. One cell free for a new patient. Sign him out, Samuel.

DR CAREW slaps MAN on the back.

Try not to shit in the streets. And do not stand by the milkmaid waiting for her to pull your udder.

DR CAREW laughs at his own joke.

SAMUEL writes in his notes. SAL takes him away.

Who do we have now?

The basketman JOHN brings in a young woman.

SAMUEL: Nancy Sprigget.

DR CAREW: Who suggested she may be fit for discharge?

MATTHEW: It was suggested to me.

DR CAREW: By whom?

MATTHEW: By Nancy, sir.

DR CAREW despairs, holds his head.

SAMUEL fumbles, takes out a tin of snuff.

DR CAREW: (*Slow, careful.*) Son, a patient in a lunatic asylum is not the person to judge his own sanity. In fact a patient is the very last person who should judge his own sanity.

NANCY: Are you the Lord?

DR CAREW: Does she sound of clear mind?

MATTHEW: She convinced me, father.

NANCY: I am a sinner, sir. I have shown my ankles to the angels who guard the gates and they will not allow me in.

DR CAREW: How long has she been here?

MATTHEW: I don't know.

DR CAREW: Samuel?

SAMUEL is distracted by his snuff.

Samuel?

SAMUEL: Two months, sir.

DR CAREW: Then how can she be recovered? Put her back in her place and apply mustard blisters after a cold bath. A purge of hellebore.

JOHN takes NANCY away.

NANCY: Where are you taking me?

JOHN: Come on.

NANCY: Take me somewhere gentle where I can hear the singing.

DR CAREW watches her go.

MATTHEW: Father.
Do you think me not apt for this profession? You are increasingly impatient with me.

DR CAREW: You are a dolt but you are my son and the Carews are the physicians in this asylum. My father was, I am, and you will be.
(*To SAMUEL.*) Could you leave the snuff to one side?

SAMUEL: Sir.

DR CAREW: Admissions?

SAMUEL: Only one today, sir.

DR CAREW: Male? Female?

SAMUEL: It is the young woman.

DR CAREW: You mean *that* young woman?

SAMUEL: Yes.

MATTHEW: What young woman?

DR CAREW: The one we have been waiting for.
Show her in.

SAL leads in MAY. They stop centre stage and DR CAREW and MATTHEW walk around her and size her up.

SAMUEL upturns his book and ink. Silence while they take her in.

DR CAREW: Well, well. For once the word was right. A true beauty indeed. A gimcrack.

MATTHEW: A chick-a-biddy.

DR CAREW: A rum blowen. Your name?

No response.

She has no tongue?

SAMUEL: Speak when the doctor speaks.

DR CAREW: Name?

MAY: May Garnett.

DR CAREW reaches out and SAMUEL passes a letter. CAREW reads.

DR CAREW: "This febrile patient's young man was sent away to sea and she was subsequently found in the orchard in a state of undress. She had such strength and force that four men had to hold her down. She vomited pieces of branches and glass which she had been consuming. She was let go of whence she ran to the pigs' trough and attempted to drown herself."
Were there no rivers? No lakes?

MAY: Sir, the water was cold and I broke the ice.

DR CAREW: It was August. I think you will find ice a rare commodity in August.

MAY: Did I do wrong? Did I stop the pig from drinking?

DR CAREW hands the notes to SAMUEL and walks around MAY.

Am I to go home now, sir? I have things to do.
Where is he?

DR CAREW: Who?

MAY: Billy.
  Where is he?

DR CAREW: He is at sea.

MAY: You tease, sir. He waits for me by the hearth.

DR CAREW: He floats upon the brine.

He turns to SAL.

Put her in with the women.

MAY: No. I must go and find him.

DR CAREW: Bleed her and bathe her.

MATTHEW: Don't shave her hair.

DR CAREW: Who is the Chief Physician?

MATTHEW: Why, you, sir. But look upon her prettiness.

MATTHEW does a little pleading dance.

She is pretty pretty pretty. Please do not. Please.

DR CAREW: Anything as long as you stop that nonsense. Do not shave her.

SAL: Sir.

DR CAREW: Dose her with laxatives. Right. All admissions done? All discharges done?

SAMUEL: Yes, sir.

DR CAREW: Good.

DR CAREW goes to leave. MATTHEW remains by MAY.

DR CAREW: Matthew. Let go of that poor lunatic and follow me.

MATTHEW: I have to?

DR CAREW: Yes.

MATTHEW lets go.

Good.

DR CAREW leaves, MATTHEW following. SAMUEL takes a last snort of snuff, packs his books and ink and leaves.

SAL and MAY remain centre stage and SAL begins to undress MAY to her underwear while the patients enter.

SCENE TWO

JOHN lays fresh straw at the entrances to the cells. The patients enter. The women include NANCY, who is always at prayer, and the delicate middle-class STELLA.

The men include RICHARD and SAMUEL. OLIVER carries his easel and palette and begins painting.

RICHARD sees MAY and rushes over, circles her. He reaches out, SAL slaps his hand.

RICHARD: Why can't I touch her? Can I touch her bubbies?

SAL: Get off.

RICHARD: She's got two bubbies.

SAL: Shut your gob.

RICHARD: Have you washed her? Is she clean? Has she got the pox? She's a rare one.

SAL: Get the water.

RICHARD gets the bucket of water. SAL roughly washes MAY.

RICHARD: Shall I take her things off? You got to wash her bubs.

SAL: Shut it.

SAL turns, hits RICHARD and he falls to the floor.

I told you to shut it.

SAL forces MAY to drink from a bottle.

Get this down.

MAY: No.

MAY struggles.

SAL: Drink.
Drink or I'll make you.

MAY drinks. JOHN runs in with a bucket and MAY vomits. SAL holds her hair back.

Take her arm.

JOHN takes her arm and SAL takes leeches from a tub and applies them.

Get sucking, boys.

RICHARD creeps up.

RICHARD: Let me suck her blood.

SAL: (*To JOHN.*) Get rid of him.

JOHN takes RICHARD's arm and drags him off to his cell, then returns.

SAL takes a blade and cuts MAY, who screams.

We got us a right noonybabby here.

MAY's arm bleeds into the bucket.

SAL: I'm hungry. I fancy a pork pie.

JOHN: Steak pie.

SAL: They ain't got the jelly.

JOHN: Pork pies ain't got the gravy.

SAL: Reckon your wife's making your steak pie now?

JOHN: No.

SAL: Oh, ain't she?

JOHN: You know she ain't.

SAL: You know what, John? You wanna be more of a man. A woman likes a man to be a man. Get her back in the kitchen.

Blood spurts over JOHN.

JOHN: Watch it. Mind what you're doing.

SAL: Oops. Sorry.

JOHN hands a bandage which SAL uses to wrap up the wound.

SAL places MAY on the straw by STELLA; JOHN helps restrain her.

SAL releases STELLA, pulls her forward.

Come on.

STELLA: I'll come. You don't have to do that.

SAL: Stand still.

SAL pulls the bucket of water towards her. She washes STELLA in cold water. RICHARD creeps out to watch.

STELLA: Please don't. I am not an animal.

RICHARD jumps to get the razor.

RICHARD: Shave her head. Go on.

JOHN: He didn't say to shave her.

RICHARD: She's diggered in lice. Make her clean. I like my women clean.

SAL: Shut up. (*Grabs her hair.*) Like a mop on washday.

STELLA: Not my hair. Please not my hair.

STELLA struggles.

JOHN: He didn't say to shave her. Rules are rules.

STELLA: Please. You're hurting me.

SAL: Am I? Ain't that a shame. A crying bleeding shame.

MAY cries out.

MAY: Billy. Billy.

STELLA: Let go of me.

NANCY emerges and sees STELLA.

NANCY: Cover up your skin.

MAY: Where am I?

NANCY: I am here to teach you the ways of the Lord. Cover your skin and embrace modesty.

SAL: Oh shut up your old clap trap. You should've thought of that when you was whoring in Covent Garden.

NANCY cries out and runs at SAL.

NANCY: The Lord is here for you.

SAL stops her and bundles her back onto the straw. RICHARD helps. JOHN moves STELLA out of the way.

SAL pulls NANCY's arms down and locks them into her metal belt.

SAL: There. Cork-brained, feather-sensed.

RICHARD: I touched her. Can I touch her again?

SAL: You ain't touching none of them.

RICHARD: Can I touch you?

SAL: Shut it.

SAL leaves. JOHN takes RICHARD back to his cell.

JOHN: Come on.

RICHARD: You got a wife to touch your sugar stick?

JOHN: Shut up.

RICHARD: How often does she touch you? My wife said I
pulled my pudding so much I made the bed jig. Made her
seasick.

JOHN: I said shut up or you want this?

JOHN shows him the gag.

RICHARD: I'll shut up.

*STELLA approaches. As she pleads, JOHN is pushing the patients
back in their cells.*

STELLA: Please. The glass is gone from the windows. The wind
drives into us. Can you get us something?

JOHN: I follow the doctor's rules. He wants you cold and quiet.

STELLA: He won't know. The new girl's young. She's ill.

JOHN: Rules are rules.

JOHN goes to leave.

STELLA: Don't go.
You know I shouldn't be in here. I'm all right. I could go
home now.

JOHN: I ain't no rule maker, love.

STELLA: I shouldn't be here. I'm not mad.

JOHN: Course you ain't. Not you. Not any of you.

NANCY: Let us place our palms together.

MAY: Is the Lord here? Where is the Lord?

STELLA: For pity's sake help.

*JOHN pushes NANCY and MAY back into the cells. He then pushes
STELLA back in.*

Let go. I'll go in.

JOHN leaves. STELLA calls out after him.

Don't go.
Don't leave us.

The patients bang on their cells with their metal plates, and rattle their chains.

SCENE THREE

Meal time. A table is erected and servants rush on with place settings and silver domed dishes. ANNABEL, a strained and puritanical woman, oversees.

DR CAREW arrives, followed as usual by MATTHEW. The men take their seats.

DR MAYNARD is shown in by a servant. MATTHEW eats slowly through the following.

DR CAREW: Ah, Doctor Maynard. How good to have your company.

DR MAYNARD: A beautiful home.

DR CAREW: Thank you. My wife's domain, I can hardly take credit. Come, come. Allow me to introduce you. My wife, Annabel. And my son Matthew, future physician of Bedlam. And this is Doctor Maynard. Bedlam's newest Governor.

DR MAYNARD: I am absolutely charmed.

DR CAREW: Have a seat. Wine?

DR MAYNARD: Only if the lady will.

ANNABEL: I'm afraid the lady is abstinent.

DR CAREW: I'm afraid the lady is an enthusiast for new licensing laws.

DR MAYNARD: Then you swim upstream in these times of excess.

DR CAREW: My wife thinks we are going to hell fast.

ANNABEL: Your wife knows we are. The evidence is not hard to come by. Streets full of drunkards. Empty churches. They are all fled to the theatres and we know what type of audience fills a theatre.

DR CAREW yawns dramatically.

DR MAYNARD: Do you go to the theatre?

DR CAREW: Do you think I am allowed? The last time I went, my wife was most displeased. I told her it was hardly risqué. A woman had written the play.

DR MAYNARD: A woman?

DR CAREW: I know. Inconceivable.

DR MAYNARD: Your wife has a point, though. The streets outside recall the decline of the Roman Empire. Perhaps time only moves in circles and society's impulses are bound to be repeated.

DR CAREW leaps up.

DR CAREW: Enough tub thumping.
Doctor, join me in a drink.

CAREW pours a glass and hands it to DR MAYNARD.

It is good of you to come.

He pours himself a glass, raises it.

To your health, Doctor, and I welcome you to the board of Governors.

They raise glasses.

It came as a surprise to have you.

DR MAYNARD: We both stumble through the alleys of the mad mind.

DR CAREW: But in very different ways.

DR MAYNARD: I like to think madness has a reason for being, that one day we may understand more.

DR CAREW: I am sure you do. (*Cold.*) My patients are contained for their good and for ours. The more they are managed, the better.
I have just admitted a young farm girl, famous for her beauty, yet she makes no sense.
What do I do with her? Allow her to return to the shit of her farmyard and drown or hang herself?

DR MAYNARD: What did you do?

DR CAREW: Blood letting. Restraints. She rests in a dark room.

DR MAYNARD: Does it work?

DR CAREW: She is alive.
We have moved on from feeding patients roasted mouse, and subjecting them to exorcism, but their state remains a mystery.
I hope you do not expect us to change the way we admit and treat our patients, Doctor, because you are now a Governor.

DR MAYNARD: I do not expect anything. I am here to observe and learn.

DR CAREW: Good.
I am proud to be from a long line of mad doctors. I know of what I speak. Whereas I believe you come from a different sort of background. Your father, I hear, was a country curate.

ANNABEL: (*Quick.*) Dr Maynard. Tell me, where did you travel from?

DR CAREW: The man does not need small talk.

DR MAYNARD: I am happy to answer.

ANNABEL: Excuse my husband. He has an increasingly weak head when he does not eat sufficient. And your temper seems to be worsening with age, does it not?

DR CAREW: The man knows of my reputation. We know what the other thinks. We have some mutual understanding, do we not?

DR MAYNARD: I think we probably do.

DR CAREW: And in the meantime, madam, do they not need supervising in the kitchen?

ANNABEL: If you feel they do.

DR CAREW: I do.

ANNABEL: Then I am sure that is the case.
(*To MAYNARD.*) Excuse me. I look forward to meeting you again.

ANNABEL leaves.

DR MAYNARD: Your wife is a charming woman.

DR CAREW: My wife, sir, is a bore.
Let us not circle the matter any more. Why are you a Governor? What do you want?

DR MAYNARD: I want merely to continue my search for the best way to help the patients make a recovery and return to their lives.

DR CAREW: Recovery? Matthew, do you hear?

MATTHEW: I listen to every word. I am an eager student, a sponge, a large ear.

DR CAREW: (*Laughs.*) Ha ha.

DR CAREW kicks MATTHEW.

MATTHEW: Father?

DR CAREW: An idiosyncratic sense of humour.

MATTHEW: What does that mean?

DR CAREW: (*Quick, embarrassed.*) Have another drink.

DR MAYNARD: I have had enough, thank you.

DR CAREW: Enough? You have not started.

CAREW pours himself a drink.

How is your private madhouse?

DR MAYNARD: Busy.

DR CAREW: The more we open, the more patients we have. Tell me, have you seen around Bedlam yet?

DR MAYNARD: Not fully.

DR CAREW: And you would like to, I imagine.

DR MAYNARD: It would be of great interest.

DR CAREW: Matthew. Would you take the doctor into Bedlam and have John show him the patients. Be sure to show him everyone. Then if you wish, Doctor Maynard, you can then return to me and explain how your new methods would improve their condition.

DR MAYNARD and MATTHEW leave with JOHN.

DR CAREW stands, calls,

DR CAREW: Get yourself in here.

PHYLLIS enters carrying a jug of gin.

Fill my glass.

Servants clear the table around them.

PHYLLIS: Where's my husband?

DR CAREW: Showing our friend the asylum. Come on. Fill my glass.

PHYLLIS: Sixpence you owe me.

DR CAREW: Is that a new dress? Your buttons gape open.

PHYLLIS: You're abnormally forward today, sir.

DR CAREW: Am I? Drip your poison into here.

PHYLLIS fills his glass.

Sit with me.

PHYLLIS points at a chair.

PHYLLIS: There?

DR CAREW pats his lap.

DR CAREW: Here? If you do not mind a hard centre to a lap.

PHYLLIS: (*Shocked.*) Sir.

PHYLLIS sits in a chair.

What has happened to you, sir?

DR CAREW: I don't know. I tire of everything today.

PHYLLIS: Are you ill?

DR CAREW: I was ill but am now healed. And am now ill again.

PHYLLIS: You are ill?

DR CAREW: I am merely tired. Come here. Sit closer. That's it.

PHYLLIS: What do you tire of?

DR CAREW: The world and its requirements. Tell me, do you think me old?

PHYLLIS: Not especially.

DR CAREW: I can not sleep.

PHYLLIS: You must sleep, sir, to get the energy for a new day.

DR CAREW: Sleep is but death and I do not have time for it. Fill my glass.

PHYLLIS: Sir. You do owe me my money.

DR CAREW: Don't bore me. One day I will talk to a woman
and she won't be wanting anything from me.

PHYLLIS: I only want what is mine.

*PHYLLIS snatches away his glass and holds up her gin bottle and
dances around.*

DR CAREW: Give me that.

PHYLLIS: When you give me my money.

DR CAREW: Come here.

PHYLLIS: Six shiny pennies.

DR CAREW: You dirty puzzle.

PHYLLIS: Dirty?

DR CAREW: A filthy trick.

PHYLLIS: I am not filthy. Do I not smell sweet as the ocean?
Sweet as the pearl within the oyster?
Show me the colour of your coins.

*CAREW gets out a pouch of money and throws it at her. PHYLLIS
picks it up, counts. She hands him the glass.*

There.

CAREW drains his glass and grabs at PHYLLIS.

DR CAREW: Come here.

PHYLLIS lifts her skirt and runs away, laughing.

Come here, you pudding bag.

CAREW chases PHYLLIS off.

SCENE FOUR

The grotto. LAURENCE strides on to centre stage. He has paper with him, and quill pen and ink. He reads out loud.

LAURENCE: *A bird's feathers do multiply the love I feel inside.*
Inside. Hide, ride, chide.
A bird's feathers do multiply this thing inside called love.
Love, dove, glove. Glove.
Oh, blow it.

LAURENCE sees GARDENIA enter.

Gardenia.
Whereon I think of you my love, my sweet,
It is ne'er too long before we two friends meet.

GARDENIA: How charming.

LAURENCE: I like to charm.
Drink?

GARDENIA: Are you not foul-headed from last night?

LAURENCE: I took a hair from the dog that bit me, and lo, I am cured.

GARDENIA: If only all of life were so simple.

LAURENCE: Ah, yes. I have been battling with language all morning.

GARDENIA: That is your occupation.

LAURENCE: A little more sympathy would be welcome. I thought you had abandoned me.

GARDENIA: As you can see I haven't.

Looks around.

It does look splendid. When do they finish?

LAURENCE: Soon, I hope. Why do you smile?

GARDENIA: Look about you. The stones of the grotto. The green of the moss. Everything is so beautiful.

LAURENCE: It would be. I designed it.
Will you stop smiling? You are too cheerful. I can't bear happiness.

GARDENIA: Listen. The birds sing as though they will have no other chance. Look about you. How can you not be happy?

LAURENCE: Happiness is all the same, like boiled oats.
You know I prefer maudlin, pale, interesting.

GARDENIA: But I am a relentless optimist.

LAURENCE: Don't even say the word. A glass is always near empty.

GARDENIA: Only because you have drunk its contents.

LAURENCE: We are entirely incompatible, are we not? Yet in this light, in this grotto, you are almost beautiful.

GARDENIA: Almost?

LAURENCE: If it were not for your advancing years, I might consider bedding you. I have not rubbed against a woman for weeks now.

GARDENIA: You will not rub against me.

LAURENCE: It is only a bit of friction, madam. One person's skin against another's.
I fear I am becoming weak with longing. I linger here in the orchard dreaming of it. I am a fruit waiting to be plucked. Waiting for a plucking. Oh for a good pluck.

GARDENIA laughs, then looks around.

Have I bored you? You look away.

GARDENIA: I only admire your grotto.

LAURENCE: You paid for it.

GARDENIA: My husband did. Late husband.

LAURENCE: Would he like it?

GARDENIA: What would he have known? He was a monumental philistine. Unlike you.

LAURENCE: *Ah. That is where our friendship lies. My friend's a genius, Gardenia cries.* Do you think I have genius?

GARDENIA: Of course I do.

LAURENCE: But how much? That is the real question I have been asking myself. Will I come close to Pope? Will I too one day have my name and visage recognised where'er I go?

GARDENIA: Is that what you desire?

LAURENCE: Yes. I desire the world to know me. To look at me. (*Sighs.*) Why did you come? Was there reason?

GARDENIA: You have forgotten, haven't you?

LAURENCE: What?

GARDENIA: It is Sunday today.

LAURENCE: You see how my mind is so full I neglect you.

GARDENIA: Will you still come?

LAURENCE: Of course. Of course.

LAURENCE and GARDENIA leave. Simultaneously SAL strides on and begins to prepare for the open Sunday at the asylum.

SCENE FIVE

Visiting day at Bedlam. SAL unlocks the restraints and NANCY, STELLA and MAY are free. SAL washes their faces and cleans the straw beds.

SAMUEL gets out the alms box and sweeps the floor, stopping for snuff. JOHN takes OLIVER down into the basement.

DR CAREW and MATTHEW enter and examine the patients.

The queue forms, including LAURENCE and GARDENIA.

During all this the NARRATOR helps PHYLLIS set up her gin barrow.

> Abroad I was walking
> One morning in the Spring,
> I heard a maid in Bedlam
> So sweetly she did sing;
> Her chains she rattled in her hands,
> And always so sang she.
>
> I love my love
> Because I know he first loved me.
>
> My love he was sent from me
> By friends that were unkind;
> They sent him far beyond the seas
> All to torment my mind.
> Although I've suffer'd for his sake,
> Content will I be, for
>
> I love my love
> Because I know he first loved me.
>
> My love he'll not come near me
> To hear the moan I make,
> And neither would he pity me
> If my poor heart should break,
> But, though I've suffer'd for his sake,
> Contented will I be, For
>
> I love my love
> Because I know he first loved me.

SAMUEL stands at the entrance with the alms box.

The NARRATOR addresses the audience.

NARRATOR: What are you doing here? You came to see the
poor lunatics? To look at them. Laugh at them.
I know what you're thinking. Thank the good Lord you
ain't in there with them.

PHYLLIS calls out, sells gin to the queue.

PHYLLIS: Sky blue.
Get yourself topsey-frizey.

NARRATOR: Brought the wife did you, sir? And you
brought your friend? And you the young grot? Lovely
entertainment for a Sunday.

PHYLLIS: Blue ruin. White satin.

PHYLLIS pours a drink for SAL and she drinks.

PHYLLIS passes drinks to the other patients.

NARRATOR: Penny each to see the lunatics.

*The visitors rush forward and put money in the box. They disperse
through the building to view the inmates.*

SAMUEL: Penny each to see the lunatics. Ladies this way.

SAMUEL hands out sticks.

*GARDENIA and LAURENCE walk towards the women. GARDENIA
stops to look at a painting. LAURENCE approaches MAY, who is apart
from the other women. LAURENCE stops, stares at MAY.*

LAURENCE: Hello.
(*Calls.*) Gardenia.

GARDENIA walks over.

Have you ever seen such beauty?

GARDENIA: Does she speak?

LAURENCE: I don't know.
Hello.
Do you hear me?

GARDENIA: She doesn't. Come.

LAURENCE: I can't leave her.
Are you unhappy? Do you have a deep sadness? I am not
put off by melancholy.
Speak to me.
Her skin so fair, her throat so fine.
This lady, Gardenia, could be mine.

MAY: My Billy has been sent away.

GARDENIA: A *country* girl. Come on.

LAURENCE: And why are you here?

MAY: I am not here.

LAURENCE: Where are you?

MAY: I am outside where the trees stretch high.
Can you not see them?

LAURENCE: I think so.

MAY: The trees grow taller with each breath I take.

LAURENCE claps.

LAURENCE: She is quite brilliant.

GARDENIA: She is quite mad.

LAURENCE: Who is Billy?

MAY: Billy is mine.

STELLA approaches. She sees LAURENCE, stops, watches.

I need to know more. Tell me more.

MAY: I am full of dry dirt. Seeds die in here.

LAURENCE: Where?

MAY shows LAURENCE the inside of her mouth.

MAY: Here.

GARDENIA sees STELLA.

STELLA steps forward. LAURENCE sees her.

STELLA: Laurence.

LAURENCE doesn't speak.

GARDENIA: Who is this woman?

LAURENCE: I don't know.

GARDENIA: She uses your name.

STELLA: It is me, Stella. I am recovered. I need you to tell them I am fine. Tell them.

GARDENIA: Why is the wretch asking you?

LAURENCE: She isn't. She is a lunatic. They are all lunatics. Mad as a bunch of pigeon milkers. Mad as a bunch of fart catchers.

STELLA: You laugh.

LAURENCE: You are entertaining.

STELLA: Am I? Am I something to mock?

GARDENIA: Who are you?

STELLA: Please help me.

LAURENCE: Do not listen. She is deluded.

STELLA grabs LAURENCE.

STELLA: Please.

LAURENCE: Get off.

SAL rushes forward.

STELLA: For God's sake, say something to her.

SAL grabs STELLA, pulls her off. STELLA screams and struggles.

Don't let her take me.

JOHN runs to help and they manhandle her off, STELLA calling out.

Don't touch me. Ask him. He'll tell you.

GARDENIA: How do you know her?

LAURENCE: I don't.

GARDENIA: How does she know your name?

LAURENCE: I don't know.

GARDENIA: I am not sure you speak the truth.

LAURENCE: Would you believe the word of a woman here over my own? Look about you. There is no reason here. No sense.

GARDENIA: Laurence.

LAURENCE: Look at them.

LAURENCE steps away. GARDENIA moves away to see the paintings.

DR CAREW approaches LAURENCE.

DR CAREW: You have been assaulted.

LAURENCE: It was nothing.

DR CAREW: I apologise. Her mind was made feeble by childbirth.

LAURENCE: Do you not describe every woman? Tell me, who is the young girl?

DR CAREW: Ah, May Garnett. She is said to be the most beautiful in London, but her mind has gone.

LAURENCE: She awakens such pity.

DR CAREW: Does she?

GARDENIA approaches. LAURENCE continues to stare at MAY.

GARDENIA: I heard of the paintings, but they are more remarkable than I conceived. Where is the artist?

DR CAREW: Locked in the basement. He is not fit for public viewing.

GARDENIA: Can I not meet him?

DR CAREW: He is not deemed suitable for ladies to view.

GARDENIA: How tantalising.

DR CAREW: I am a tantalising man.

GARDENIA: Then why don't you take me to look at him. I am intrigued.

DR CAREW: But not of a nervous disposition?

GARDENIA: Do I seem it?

DR CAREW: No.

GARDENIA: Then take me down. I note your donations box and if I were moved, I might feel inclined to offer financial help for your poor patients.

DR CAREW laughs.

DR CAREW: You are persuasive.

GARDENIA: I am a woman and you are a man.

DR CAREW: Follow me.

GARDENIA follows DR CAREW. LAURENCE stops, looks back at MAY. GARDENIA calls.

GARDENIA: Laurence.

LAURENCE follows and they go down into the cellar.

Visitors move towards the women patients and RICHARD hands them a stick.

RICHARD: Poke them. She likes a poke. Poke poke. Harder.

A MAN pokes NANCY who stands.

MAN: What day is it?

NANCY: The day the Lord speaks and announces a new beginning.

MAN: Give us a kiss, love.

NANCY: My friends, the Lord has asked me to speak with you.

RICHARD jumps up and down.

RICHARD: Touch her. Go on. Touch her.

ANNABEL arrives. She watches for a while, anger mounting.

MAN: Ask her something.

WOMAN: Who are your friends?

NANCY: These are the angels which clean me, and stand by my side.

MAN: Let's see your drawers.

NANCY: They are not for human eyes.

MAN: God said I should see them.

NANCY: He speaks to you?

MAN: He sends me messages. He said you would show me your legs.

NANCY: God said that?

NANCY pulls her dress up slowly revealing her legs and pants.

ANNABEL: Stop.

ANNABEL snatches the stick.

Leave her alone.

MAY is getting agitated.

Please all of you, go home.

MAN: I paid a penny for me, a penny for her.

RICHARD: I saw her legs. (*Dances around MAN.*) I saw her drawers.

RICHARD grabs the WOMAN.

Can I touch your bubs?

WOMAN screams and pushes him away.

Do you suck him? Do you do it to him?

MAN: Come here.

MAN steps forward and tries to fight RICHARD, who dances around.

DR MAYNARD steps out from the crowd.

DR MAYNARD: Enough. Leave them alone.

MAN: We want our money back.

DR MAYNARD: Go on. Go. Get out. All of you.

The crowd disperse.

ANNABEL: Dr Maynard.

DR MAYNARD: Mrs Carew.

ANNABEL: Thank you.

STELLA approaches.

STELLA: Sir. Madam.
Please hear me out. Please. Someone must listen. I had a baby and did lose my mind but I have since regained it.

NANCY jumps at STELLA.

NANCY: Don't talk to a man. Your eyes will bleed.
God will say you are unclean.

DR MAYNARD and ANNABEL help pull NANCY off.

SAL and JOHN approach quickly. SAL bundles NANCY back. JOHN holds STELLA.

STELLA: Help me.

DR MAYNARD: Go gentle on her. She was not harming us.

STELLA: Not back there. No. Do not allow them to do this.

SAL and JOHN drag STELLA to the restraints.

PHYLLIS approaches with gin.

PHYLLIS: Ease your heart. Come on, your best Geneva.

PHYLLIS sees ANNABEL, stops.

ANNABEL: You can peddle that outside.

PHYLLIS: Lady, have a bit on me. It's only a bit of fun, rid us of the grey skies.

DR MAYNARD: Sell it outside.

PHYLLIS: What's a poor woman to do for money, sir? Are you expecting me to fall back on myself?

DR MAYNARD: Get out.

PHYLLIS leaves.

ANNABEL: (*To SAL and JOHN.*) Lock up these women and leave them in peace.

SAL: All cells are to be open today.

DR MAYNARD: Lock them up.

SAL: Governor.

JOHN: Lock them in.

SAL moves away. She and JOHN lock up the women.

ANNABEL: My husband's approach appears to deteriorate further each time I come.

DR MAYNARD: It is not an approach I admire.

ANNABEL: You have no need to use such cautious language. I hope you will report this to the other Governors.

DR MAYNARD: I will report all that I see.

ANNABEL: I trust you to tell the truth as you see it. Now excuse me for I think I have spoken out enough against my own husband.

DR MAYNARD: Madam.

ANNABEL moves away and leaves DR MAYNARD, who watches her go, then goes to the patients and examines how they are restrained and their living conditions. SAMUEL counts the money from the alms box.

DR CAREW appears from the cellar with OLIVER, who is heavily restrained, and sees DR MAYNARD. He approaches, taking OLIVER with him.

DR CAREW: Dr Maynard.

DR MAYNARD: Good afternoon.

DR CAREW: I had no word that you would be here with us today.

DR MAYNARD: The institution is open to anyone.

DR CAREW: If they pay their penny.

DR MAYNARD: If that is what concerns you, I have paid it.

DR CAREW: It all goes to our wretches. As you can see, they are in need.

DR MAYNARD: This is?

DR CAREW: You know, of course.

OLIVER: Good afternoon to you.

DR MAYNARD: Good afternoon. Are these restraints not tight?

OLIVER: A little. They pinch the skin.

DR CAREW: He is fine.

DR MAYNARD: How do you fare here?

OLIVER: I need people to talk to.

DR MAYNARD: I see. Can he not have people?

DR CAREW: No.

OLIVER: Have you seen my paintings?

DR MAYNARD: Not yet.

OLIVER: I could show you them if you like.

DR MAYNARD: That would be of great interest, thank you.

OLIVER: You will need a hat, sir. They communicate through
your hair, you see. They send messages through the
follicles.

DR CAREW calls out.

DR CAREW: John.

JOHN approaches.

OLIVER: You could come down with me.

DR CAREW: I think another time. John? Give him a laxative
and a cold bath.

JOHN: Doctor.

JOHN takes OLIVER to the cell.

DR MAYNARD: Do you yet have an understanding of why he
did it?

DR CAREW: An understanding? They found joints upon
the butcher's block. A knife so sharp the whetstone was
blunt. A pan with half his sister's head in, fully poached.

An unclean napkin. What kind of understanding did you imagine we might have?

DR MAYNARD: Something caused him to do it.

DR CAREW: Did it?

DR MAYNARD: Otherwise we might all do it.

DR CAREW: My task is not to analyse insanity, but to protect the world from him and him from his own self.

DR MAYNARD: In that case how does it help to have the public enter and view him? Or indeed any of these patients?

DR CAREW: They feel less than the dogs out in the street. And we need the money it brings. I hope you are not attempting to preach to me, Maynard. I will not listen.

DR CAREW sees the women locked away.

John? John? Who ordered the cells to be locked.

JOHN: Your wife, sir.

DR CAREW: Did she?

JOHN appears.

John. Undo the cells. It is visiting day.

JOHN: If that is what you want? Yes, sir.

JOHN begins unlocking the cells and releasing patients.

DR MAYNARD: Doctor, I have some questions for you.

DR CAREW takes the alms box from SAMUEL and begins to count.

DR CAREW: Your questions can wait. This gentleman's finished here now. Show him the gate, the visit is over. Now.

SAMUEL: Sir.

SAMUEL shows DR MAYNARD out.

DR CAREW: I need a drink. Where is she?

DR CAREW leaves.

SCENE SIX

Vauxhall Pleasure Gardens. Evening. There is music and people parade and stare.

The BEDLAMITES stroll on, accompanied by masked promenading socialites.

PHYLLIS arrives with her gin.

LAURENCE waits, watches as a man holds a bear on a leash. People bait it and the bear steps forward and undresses and a WOMAN emerges.

GARDENIA finally arrives. Their conversation is interrupted by onlookers and musicians.

LAURENCE: I thought you were coming an hour ago.

GARDENIA: The boat was full, I had to wait for another.

LAURENCE: I thought these Vauxhall Pleasure Gardens.

GARDENIA: They are.

LAURENCE: Where is the pleasure?

GARDENIA: Around you. Look how happy the world is. Don't you be ill tempered.

LAURENCE: I am pining.

GARDENIA: For whom?

LAURENCE: You know for whom. You saw her in that fearful place.

GARDENIA: Not the lunatic.

LAURENCE has a thought. A man pushes a woman in a barrow through them, weaves around.

LAURENCE: You are jealous of her.

GARDENIA: No.

LAURENCE: It is because she is young and fresh and unspoilt.

GARDENIA: I am not jealous of a young girl.

LAURENCE: The more you say you are not and the more you spit out the words young girl, the more I know you are.

GARDENIA: To be jealous I would have to want you for myself which I do not.

LAURENCE: That is what you say.

GARDENIA: Do not flatter yourself, friend. Anyway, the young girl is mad.

LAURENCE: Do not say the word mad.

GARDENIA: Mad.

LAURENCE: No.

GARDENIA: Mad. Mad. Mad.

LAURENCE: You are as bad as Stella.

GARDENIA: Stella?

LAURENCE: Nothing.

GARDENIA: Stella? In Bedlam?

LAURENCE: I didn't say that.

GARDENIA: I knew you knew her.
A mistress?

LAURENCE: Once upon a time.

GARDENIA: I see.

LAURENCE: She was beautiful once. Before she went mad.

GARDENIA: Was it your child?

LAURENCE: She claimed so.

GARDENIA: It was.

LAURENCE: They all look the same.

GARDENIA: Why did you not acknowledge her?

LAURENCE: I didn't recognise her.

GARDENIA: I don't believe you.

LAURENCE: I had just seen May and been hit with a massive affliction. I am open to experiences that others do not feel. When a poet falls in love, believe me, he falls a long, long way.

GARDENIA: And when a poet tires of his mistress?

LAURENCE: I have had enough of this subject.

GARDENIA: You have to do something for her.

LAURENCE: Do I? I, my lady, am much involved, much concerned with attempting to capture my feelings towards May Garnett in language.

GARDENIA: And Stella? Is she to stay there and rot?

LAURENCE: Look, Gardenia, the lady is clearly ill and is in good hands. The best hands in the best place. There is nothing I can do.

GARDENIA: But she asked for help. She sounded sane.

LAURENCE: Do not trust the word of a madwoman.

GARDENIA: But you say you love a madwoman.

LAURENCE: That is different.
    Did you come all this way to fight with me?

GARDENIA: No.

LAURENCE: Then let us not fight. We have things to celebrate. We are here in Vauxhall, we have each other as friends. And I have met the most beautiful girl in the entire country.

Music starts up. The masked socialites leave and the following street scene begins to build.

GARDENIA: And Stella?

LAURENCE: Leave it to me.

GARDENIA: You will do something?

LAURENCE: Yes.

GARDENIA: You give me your word?

LAURENCE: I do. I give you my solemn word.
Enough of this seriousness.
Come, let us have a drink and toast today. Let us toast new loves and friends and the future. Let us toast this exact hour. No. Let us toast this exact minute, this second. Let us toast now. The nowness of now.

LAURENCE grabs a gin from PHYLLIS and hands one to GARDENIA. They touch glasses and drink, then step into the boat and leave.

SCENE SEVEN

Night. Street scene, St Giles. PHYLLIS is with her gin barrow and pours glasses to sell. The BEDLAMITES stagger on.

PHYLLIS: St Giles. Nights are like life. Dark and short and brutal. And gin is like your mother: it's Madam Geneva what wakes you, warms you, puts you to bed.

NARRATOR: We scratch at the earth, sing a few songs, and reach out our upturned palms.

PHYLLIS: Kick in the guts. Strip me naked.

NARRATOR: Do I have to? Know what? There's one thing what living on the streets teaches you. That's all about people. We know them all. We know those who've known the ups and the downs, the feather beds and the pavements. They'll hand us a penny, tell us to enjoy our drink.

PHYLLIS hands him a drink.

Cheers.

Then there's those who'll turn their horse to the puddle in the hope of drowning us. And the worst of them all's the pious ones, those that'll buy us food but not trust us with pennies in case we buy a bit of liquid comfort.

PHYLLIS refills his drink.

Liquid. Comfort.

The BEDLAMITES clap and stamp as he downs it in one. He sings with PHYLLIS.

Drinkers drift on and buy gin and join in the song.

SONG: As I went home on Monday night,
    As drunk as I could be,
    I went into the stable,
    and there for me to see,
    A saddled horse a-standing,
    As patient as can be.

    I called out to my loving wife,
    'O what does this horse here?'
    'Why, you drunk, you drunk, you silly old drunk,
    can't you very well see?
    This is but a milking-cow,
    my mother sent to me.'
    'Heyday! Godzounds! A milking-cow with bridle and saddle on!
    the like was never known!'

    As I went home on Tuesday night,
    As drunk as I could be,
    I went into the kitchen,
    and there for me to see,
    A silver sword a-hanging,
    As sharp as sharp can be.

I called out to my loving wife,
'O what does this sword here?'
'Why, you drunk, you drunk, you silly old drunk,
can't you very well see?
It is but a roasting-spit,
my mother sent to me.'
'Heyday! Godzounds! A roasting spit with a scabbard on!
the like was never known!'

As I went home on Wednesday night,
As drunk as I could be,
I went into the pantry,
and there for me to see,
A pair of boots were hanging,
As dirty as can be.

I called out to my loving wife,
'O what do these boots do here?'
'Why, you drunk, you drunk, you silly old drunk,
can't you very well see?
They are two pudding-bags,
my mother sent to me.'
'Heyday! Godzounds! Pudding-bags with spurs on!
the like was never known!'

As I went home on Thursday night,
As drunk as I could be,
I went into my chamber,
and there for me to see,
In bed a man was lying,
As handsome as could be.

I called out to my loving wife,
'O what does this man in bed with you?'
'Why, you drunk, you drunk, you silly old drunk,
don't you very well see?
He is a pretty milking-maid,
my mother sent to me.'
'Heyday! Godzounds! A milking-maid with a beard on!
the like was never known!'

You drunk, you drunk, you silly old drunk,
Don't you very well see?

Drinkers approach.

PHYLLIS: There you go, my darling. You enjoy it while you
can remember where you are.
Tip your head well back.

A young man, BILLY, approaches.

Here, lad. Sluice your gob. Penny a go.

BILLY: I ain't got no money.

PHYLLIS: They all say that, my love. Everyone's a got a penny.

BILLY: I ain't.

PHYLLIS: A halfpenny.

BILLY: Honest. I'm broke as a stone.

PHYLLIS: You ain't from London.

BILLY: I'm looking for someone.

PHYLLIS: May as well search for a minnow in the ocean. Go
on. Have it on me.

PHYLLIS passes him the drink, pours herself one.

BILLY drinks, chokes on it. PHYLLIS laughs.

A gin virgin, were you?

BILLY: Ain't tasted it like that.

PHYLLIS: Now you know what you been missing.

PHYLLIS pours him some more.

Who you looking for?

BILLY: My girl.

PHYLLIS: London's a big place to look. You want to watch
your back talking like you do. And your front and sides.

There's gangs hang round the theatres. Ain't safe nowhere. Knives they got and they'll slice you to get your money.

BILLY: I may sound stupid but I ain't. Been seeing the world.

PHYLLIS: Big, was it?

BILLY: Course it was. Got back last week.

PHYLLIS: Found your sea legs, did you?

BILLY: Sick every day to begin.

PHYLLIS: Where you resting your nut?

BILLY: Ain't resting nowhere.

PHYLLIS: You want to get hold of some money and I can find you a nice bed for a few days. Nice soft blousy to share it with.

BILLY: I don't want a blousy. I'm looking for my girl.

PHYLLIS: There's plenty of girls to go round.

BILLY: Don't want plenty. I want mine. Mine is the most beautiful girl you ever seen.

PHYLLIS: Course she is. Long as she's got two legs, two eyes and all her things in the right places. I know what you lads are. You don't look at the mantelpiece when you poke the fire.

PHYLLIS reaches out for his glass.

You gonna find some money and have another?

BILLY: I ain't got none.

PHYLLIS: Please yourself.

PHYLLIS calls out.

Kill-grief. Heart's ease. Kick in the guts. Strip me naked.

DR CAREW approaches drunkenly.

DR CAREW: I'll strip you naked.

PHYLLIS: Doctor.

DR CAREW: Let us feel your dairy.

PHYLLIS clutches her bosom.

PHYLLIS: Feel your own wife.

DR CAREW: Give us a drink.

PHYLLIS holds the drink out of reach.

PHYLLIS: What colour's your money.

DR CAREW hands over a coin.

DR CAREW: Get one for the young man.

BILLY: Thank you, sir. That's generous. Cheers.

They drink.

Can you tell me where I am?

DR CAREW: You're in London.

PHYLLIS: Where you going?

BILLY: East.

DR CAREW spins drunkenly, points everywhere.

DR CAREW: That way's east.

PHYLLIS: That way.

DR CAREW: That way.

PHYLLIS: Listen, lad. That way.

BILLY: City's too big for me.

PHYLLIS: Big enough to drive you mad, ain't it?

DR CAREW: Who's mad?

PHYLLIS: No-one. You're off duty now.

DR CAREW: Am I? Have another.

BILLY: I daren't, sir. My head's like sheep wool as it is. Thanks, sir, for the drink.

BILLY leaves. PHYLLIS calls out.

PHYLLIS: Good luck.

PHYLLIS turns to DR CAREW.

It's way past cock shut time.

DR CAREW: I can't sleep.

PHYLLIS: You should be in bed with your wife.

DR CAREW: Another drink.

PHYLLIS holds out her hand. CAREW gives her money and she fills his drink.

Raises glass.

Cheers.

PHYLLIS: To your health.

DR CAREW: Not much left, I'm afraid.

PHYLLIS: Maybe I better take that off you.

DR CAREW: It'll do me good.

PHYLLIS: What you doing here, Doctor? What's here for you?

DR CAREW: I don't know.

PHYLLIS: Are you all right, sir?

DR CAREW: Yes. Tell me something. Do you turn your back on your husband? Do you let him butter your buns?

PHYLLIS: Have you had a few?

DR CAREW: I've not been well.

PHYLLIS: Drinking here ain't gonna help.

DR CAREW: Talk to me.

PHYLLIS: What d'you want to talk about?

DR CAREW: I've not been a good husband.

PHYLLIS: You can start now.

DR CAREW: Too late.

DR CAREW places down his drink and begins to move towards her.

You have fine hot blood.

PHYLLIS: My heart pumps it to all corners of my body, sir. What has entered you, sir?

DR CAREW: I don't know.

PHYLLIS: You are not yourself.

DR CAREW: Then who am I?
Come to me.

PHYLLIS: Your breathing is heavy, sir. Doctor, are you with fever?

DR CAREW: Fever, yes. Feel my head.

She feels him. He grabs her hand and pushes it to his trousers.

Lower, madam. Lower.
Ah, yes.
Let me roam through your narrow streets. Let me swim on your river. Let me address the crowds in your marketplace. Your arms are Bishopsgate. Your head Covent Garden. Your waist the ribbon of the River Thames. You are my own London.

They kiss and CAREW lifts her skirts.

PHYLLIS: Sir. Sir.

DR CAREW: Come. Let us seek a doorway. There is more to the night than this.

PHYLLIS and DR CAREW move away and we see his bare behind as they begin to have sex in a doorway.

The DRINKERS help themselves to gin from the barrow, then push it off.

Night ends and the new day breaks.

SCENE EIGHT

Bedlam. The moon leaves, the cock crows and the birds call out: dawn has arrived.

The WASHERWOMEN empty the night soil from chamber pots.

A woman cries out and SAL walks through the ward. She meets MATTHEW.

MATTHEW: The sun is creeping up.

SAL: That's what the sun does.

MATTHEW: It creeps.

SAL: It rises as the moon goes down.

MATTHEW: How incredible. Like a pair of scales. Like this. Like this. Is that how it is?

SAL: Sort of. What did you think happened?

MATTHEW: I am not sure it's something I have thought about.

SAL: Do you think?

MATTHEW: Sometimes. I hear these voices in my head. Is that what thinking is?

SAL: You have something in common with our patients.

MATTHEW: Do you think so?

SAL: Oh dear. Shall we start again?

MATTHEW: Start what again?

SAL: Can we pretend we are seeing each other for the first time?

MATTHEW: If you would like to.

MATTHEW claps, excited.

This is fun. I am walking here and I say:
The sun is creeping up.

SAL: And I say that is because it is morning. And then I say, I am here because I thought I heard someone cry out.

MATTHEW: There was no cry. You can go back now.

SAL: But now it is too late.

SAL gets out a bottle, pours a drink. She offers it to MATTHEW.

Fancy a drop? It'll wake you up.

MATTHEW: Will it?

MATTHEW drinks.

You're right. I feel really awake now.

SAL: What are you doing here, doctor?

MATTHEW: I'm no doctor.

SAL: You will be.

MATTHEW: I don't know. I don't think I have the mind for it.

SAL: What mind d'you mean?

SAL impersonates DR CAREW.

Come come, let us see the patients. What do we have here? A woman hearing voices and biting her own arms. Take her away. Blister her with mustard, dose her with hellebore till she shits between her teeth and the bucket's full of vomit. Give her a bath cold enough to make her toothypegs dance. Tie her arms down and place her in the dark. Laxatives, laxatives, laxatives. Get the bowels open.

That's what we need, a nice clean bowel. Good, good. Run along now, we do not have time for speculation, indolence.

MATTHEW: That's rather good.

SAL: All you got to do is read the notes and decide which of his bag of tricks they'll have. If in doubt give them all.

MATTHEW: You make it sound quite simple.

SAL: They just make it sound more than it is, or they wouldn't get the money for it. Believe me, he don't know what he's doing any more than I know.

MAY moans.

SAL: That's the cry I heard.

MATTHEW: It's May.

MAY moves and wakes and stands.

MAY: Where am I?

SAL: You're still here.

MAY: The moon is bright on us and I couldn't sleep.
    You have come with news?
    I hear the sea. I see the waves.

She sings.

My one love, my true love, my boy from the sea,
He left me behind and he whispered to me,
"My one love, my sweet love, take a lock of my hair,
One day I'll be back and I'll make us a pair."

MAY begins to cry.

I want to go home.
Someone take me home where I know the air by the smell
and I can lay upon my feather bed.
Where I breathe with the waves and I know myself.
Please.

MAY looks around and still half crying, begins to laugh.

She looks at MATTHEW.

Come here. Will you touch me.

MATTHEW goes to move forward. SAL grabs him.

MAY pulls up her nightdress and slips her hand into her pants.

Touch me.

SAL steps forward, stops MAY.

SAL: Stop that.

MAY: Don't come near me. Don't touch me.

MATTHEW steps forward.

Who are you?

MATTHEW: I am the doctor.

MAY gasps.

MAY: Billy. You are my Billy returned to me.

SAL: No.

SAL gets herself between MAY and MATTHEW.

NANCY wakes, gets up.

NANCY: What is it?

MAY: He's come. He's here.

NANCY: Is he come? Is he here to save us all?
He is here to guide us and he will pour his words on us as
warm oil.
Oh, Lord. Hallelujah.

MAY: Billy. Let me touch you.

SAL: No touching the doctor.

STELLA wakes.

STELLA: What is it? Why is he here?

MAY: He is my Billy.

STELLA: (*To SAL.*) He's always here. (*To MATTHEW.*) I know what you're doing.

SAL: Get back to sleep or I'll dose you. Go on. Get back. All of you.

SAL tries to push them back.

STELLA: No.

SAL: I warn you.

MAY: Talk to me of love, Billy.
Come to me.

MAY embraces MATTHEW.

STELLA: It is not your Billy.

MAY: Why this is my Billy.

MAY licks his face.

He tastes of the sea.
Touch me, Billy.

MATTHEW: She wants to be touched. She asked me.

SAL: No.

MATTHEW: But I have never touched a woman.

SAL drags MATTHEW off.

MAY: Billy. Come to me.

SAL: Run, doctor.

As they struggle, DR CAREW returns, drunk, propped up by the equally drunk PHYLLIS.

MATTHEW: Father? You aren't come to work.

DR CAREW: I am.

MATTHEW: You're not fit.

DR CAREW: Fit? I have never been fitter nor brighter nor more equipped for this foul world.

MATTHEW: You're drunk.

DR CAREW: Smell my breath.

MATTHEW steps close and smells.

MATTHEW: I think you should go home.

DR CAREW: Home? Christ you are your mother's son. I need to see my patients. I do not need the help of an incompetent noodle. Where is the beauty? Come on. (*Starts banging a rhythm and sings.*) For what am I waiting? What am I waiting?

SAMUEL brings on the desk and book and ink and sets up his office. JOHN and SAL follow on. JOHN sees PHYLLIS.

JOHN: What are you doing here?

PHYLLIS: The doctor. I brought him back.

DR CAREW: The beauty. Get her up. Up.

MATTHEW: She is up.

DR CAREW: Where?

MATTHEW: Behind you.

DR CAREW looks round and falls over.

MATTHEW helps him up.

DR CAREW: I'm not a bloody invalid. Where is she?

SAL brings MAY and stands her in front of him.

Ah. Here you are. There are so many of you. Stop moving.

MAY: I move with the waves.

DR CAREW: You're mad. You don't make sense.

MATTHEW: Father, allow me to take over.

DR CAREW: Don't be so absurd.
We do not have time for speculation, indolence. Matthew, what have you seen?

MATTHEW: I saw her with her hand in her drawers.

DR CAREW: Strengthens the arm but softens the brain. The cause of sterility, impotence and pimples. Apply leeches to her.

SAL: Down below, doctor?

MATTHEW: Will it not hurt her?

DR CAREW: She feels no pain. She feels no cold. She feels no hunger.
She is mad, and she is a woman. It is double the blow.

MAY: Sir. My mind is puzzled and I feel it spinning.
Am I a nuisance?

DR CAREW: Oh, shut up.
I have had enough of this. Your symptoms are all the same. You are all beyond help.

DR CAREW kicks SAMUEL.

All of you, you are all mad.
Where is the music? Music. I need music. Drink. I need drink.

The BEDLAMITES begin to play. PHYLLIS pours DR CAREW a drink.

The patients rattle their chains and bang their plates, and shout and cry.

DR CAREW grabs PHYLLIS and begins to dance. RICHARD watches then tries to push DR CAREW away and dance with PHYLLIS.

RICHARD: Let me. Let me.

DR CAREW: She's mine.

RICHARD: I want her.

They begin to fight over her as NANCY emerges and stands centre.

NANCY: My dearly beloved, we are gathered here today in this
house of the Lord.

*RICHARD grabs MAY and makes her dance. MAY screams and fights
him off.*

The Lord made all of these things and he did not make
them for us to darken them. We are to remain upright and
never touch a person who wishes to touch us in an intimate
place.

*OLIVER emerges from the cellar and creeps up behind MAY, watches
her.*

MAY: Billy. Where is Billy?

DR CAREW: He is riding the waves.

*MATTHEW takes MAY, pulls her. RICHARD also pulls her and she is
stretched out between them.*

STELLA comes out.

STELLA: Stop it.

She pulls RICHARD and MATTHEW off MAY.

Leave her alone. All of you, leave her alone.

DR CAREW: John, take this woman away. Lock her up. She
tries to stop us.

JOHN: Perhaps it's for a reason.

DR CAREW: A reason? Getting a bit important, aren't we?
Don't you become a bore as well. Go and join my wife in
her desiccated life. Go on.

DR CAREW dances, takes MAY's arm. STELLA tries to stop him.

Take her away.

STELLA is taken away.

Let us have another drink.

PHYLLIS goes to get some more gin.

RICHARD: Can it be my turn. Can I dance with her and hold her tightly.

DR CAREW: She is mine. You are all mine.

DR CAREW grabs RICHARD. He dances with him.

MATTHEW: Father, you dance with a man.

DR CAREW: Son, you are a genius.

You clod hopping fool. That was my toe.

NANCY: The Lord will not like it.

DR CAREW: The Lord can whistle for his gin.

Come. Dance.

DR CAREW grabs NANCY and dances with her.

LAURENCE enters, holding his papers.

LAURENCE: Sir.

DR CAREW stops and fakes a collapse.

DR CAREW: Shut the gates and rid us of these people.

LAURENCE: I have come to give this linguistic gift to May Garnett.

LAURENCE unravels a poem, begins to read.

To you I come with bended knees and pleading eyes,
I pledge to you my art, my love, knowing it never dies.

DR CAREW: (*Shouts.*) Gallery maid, rid us of this man.

LAURENCE: Sir, your manner leaves much to be desired. I bring only a work to be delivered to the fair young lady.

DR CAREW: You pompous arse. Pompous arsicle. Arsicle parsicle. Arse parcel.
Music. Let us have more music.

The BEDLAMITES play.

Not that one. Another.

The BEDLAMITES stop, start again.

Do you dance?

LAURENCE: If I have no choice.

DR CAREW: You have none.

LAURENCE: Sir. I must plead with you.

DR CAREW: Must you? I hate pleading.

LAURENCE: I need time alone with May.

DR CAREW: Why?

LAURENCE: I love her.

DR CAREW: How can you love her?

DR CAREW dances, finishes a drink, then turns back to Laurence.

I think it time for you to go.

LAURENCE: I can not leave my love.

OLIVER stalks closer to MAY.

DR CAREW: You can.

LAURENCE: I can't.

DR CAREW: I said you are to leave. Now. Now. Now.

DR CAREW chases him and LAURENCE throws down the papers and is escorted away by SAL.

DR CAREW picks up the papers, imitates;

To you I come with bended knees and pleading eyes,
I pledge to you my art, my love, knowing it never dies.
Pompous poeting herring gutted jingle brains.
Where is that woman?

PHYLLIS steps forward.

JOHN: That is my wife.

DR CAREW: She is a sauce box. And she is mine.

JOHN steps forward. MATTHEW leaps between them.

MATTHEW: He doesn't mean it.

DR CAREW: I do.

They begin to fight.

RICHARD, SAMUEL and MATTHEW separate them.

PHYLLIS: Let's all have a drink.

PHYLLIS gets drinks.

OLIVER grabs MAY and she screams. They all stop. OLIVER holds out a knife.

OLIVER: She's mine.

OLIVER moves towards the cellar and puts the knife to her neck.

Get back.
I said get back.

DR CAREW: Have a drink with us.

RICHARD: Let her go.

OLIVER: Dance. Music. I said music.

The music begins.

OLIVER beckons at DR CAREW.

Go on. Dance. Dance.

DR CAREW dances.

All of you. Follow him. Go on. Over there.

They all link up and dance off. OLIVER strokes MAY's hair and takes her down into the cellar. The door bangs behind him.

Act Two

PROLOGUE

Gin Lane. Street scene outside Bedlam.

A woman lets her baby fall: a man chews a bone. A woman feeds her baby gin. Another man in a barrow is fed gin by a woman.

A MAN appears on the upper balcony and pisses down onto the stage. He is seen and jeered at and is chased away.

PHYLLIS pours coloured liquid into bottles of gin.

PHYLLIS: Mind fire. Diddle. Frog's wine. Rag water.
Sweetened, unsweetened. Stirred into ale. Parliamentary brandy. Get it here.
Flavoured gins for your sweet tooth. Aniseed, juniper, elderberries, cherries, raspberries.

PHYLLIS passes the NARRATOR rags and they dip them in the bottles, and set fire to them, testing their proof.

PHYLLIS: Look at the strength of this. Check the proof.
All that lovely alcohol.

The BEDLAMITES sing.

As Oyster Nan stood by her tub,
To show her vicious inclination;
She gave her noblest parts a scrub,
And sigh'd for want of copulation:
A vintner of no little fame,
Who excellent red and white can sell ye,
Beheld the dirty little dame,
As she stood scratching of her belly.

'Come in,' says he, 'you silly slut,
Tis now a rare convenient minute,
I'll lay the itching of your scut,

Except some greedy Devil be in it.'
With that the flat-capt Fusby smiled,
And would have blush'd, but that she could not;
'Alas,' says she, 'we're soon beguil'd
By men who do those things we should not.'

From door they went behind the bar,
As it's by common fame reported;
And there upon a Turkey chair,
Unseen the loving couple sported;
But being called by company,
As he was taking pains to please her,
'I'm coming, coming, sir,' says he,
'My dear, and so am I,' says she, sir.

Her mole-hill belly swell'd about,
Into a mountain quickly after;
And when the pretty mouse crept out,
The creature caus'd a mighty laughter:
And now she has learnt the pleasing game,
Although much pain and shame it cost her,
She daily ventures at the same,
And shuts and opens like an oyster.

NARRATOR: Thank you. Thank you.
Enough. Enough. Out out. Go on. Out.

The chaos clears.

(*To AUDIENCE, begging*) Thank you. Thank you. Very kind,
sir.

Now I got something to tell you all.
I wasn't always Tom o'Bedlam.
I was a rich man once. I wore a wig that touched the
ceiling and swept away the cobwebs. I slept between silk
sheets on top of swan feathers.
I made my money myself and the only thing that dirtied
my hands was the ink on the notes. Know how I did it?
Trading in South Sea shares, up and down Exchange Alley.

DOCTOR MAYNARD enters, followed by a crowd. People drift to listen to him. He holds up his pamphlet.

DR MAYNARD: Ladies and gentlemen. For too long London's mad have been treated by a small number of people in privileged posts. They have been secretive and protectionist, and reneged on their moral duty to educate the next generation of mad doctors.

It is time for a new approach, and to this end, I am publishing my views.

NARRATOR: The excitement of trading made gin look like a sleeping draught.

The gamble, the scent of blood. Buy for one hundred, but do I hold my position and wait for five hundred? Or do I sell at two hundred and reinvest? The heart beats hard and the breath pants and perspiration smears the upper lip.

DR MAYNARD: It has always been believed that all madness is the same, and requires the same limited treatment. But I argue in this publication that we can identify two types. There is original madness, there at birth, incurable. But there is also another form of madness, caused by an external event. This might be childbirth, illness, unrequited love, or something like the loss of a fortune. Yes, that is sufficient to throw the balance of the mind.

NARRATOR: I bought and sold, reinvested. I lay upon my swan feather bed and watched the prices rise, counted up what I was worth. Oh there was drinking, I confess, and a bit of the other. The old oyster diving. Then, the bubble began to stretch and pull until one day it burst and the share price fell.

The first thing to go were the horses, then the carriage. The wife packed her dresses and her powders and potions, and left a note. The man came for the house key. And then, when I had nothing more to lose, this started to go.

DR MAYNARD: My words will not be popular with all, but I am making necessary progress, and I believe we stand at the beginning of a new period in the study of madness and the treatment of the insane.

One day, I hope, we will look back upon the current asylums and express horror at our brutal treatment of the ill.

Thank you.

DR MAYNARD hands out books.

NARRATOR: And so I took to the streets, raving and railing against all who offered help, until I was brought to my knees and then taken through the gates we all dread. Bedlam.

SCENE ONE

Bedlam. Afternoon.

JOHN stands with MATTHEW by the cellar door.

JOHN lies down, puts his ear on the floor.

MATTHEW: What can you hear?

John?

JOHN: Shhh.

JOHN listens.

MATTHEW: Well?

JOHN: While you are talking, sir, I can't hear nothing.

MATTHEW: Oh. I see. *(Laughs.)* Of course. Now?

JOHN: You are still talking, sir.

MATTHEW: So I am. Can you hear anything now?

JOHN: You still are.

MATTHEW places his own hand over his mouth, gesticulates wildly.

I don't understand.

MATTHEW removes his hand with his other hand.

MATTHEW: I was just trying to say, I won't say anything.

JOHN: Then stand still and be silent.

MATTHEW: I'll try.

JOHN listens.

JOHN: No. I can't hear anything.

MATTHEW: Do you think I should go in?

JOHN: I'm not sure you'd come out, sir.

MATTHEW: I know. Perhaps we should both go in. I could stand in front and wave my arms, much like a decoy, and you could run at him from behind.

JOHN: But he will have seen me enter.

MATTHEW: Ah yes. How about the window?

JOHN: If we go in by the windows he'll know and if we go in through the doors he'll know.

MATTHEW: I see.
Hmm. This is a difficult dilemma.

MATTHEW thinks.

Can I ask you something?

JOHN: Of course, sir.

MATTHEW: You managed to get a wife.

JOHN: Of sorts.

MATTHEW: I would like a wife.

JOHN: I think they're over-rated, sir.

MATTHEW: Really?

JOHN: Well, sir, see it like this. Imagine if you bought a new feather bed. You're allowed to sleep on it occasionally but the rest of the time it chases you around and tells you what to do.

MATTHEW: Eek.

JOHN: That's what it's like.

MATTHEW: But at least you get to lie on it a few times. My bed so far is unslept in, if you catch my meaning.

JOHN: I think I do, sir, but we should attend to the matter in hand.

MATTHEW: I should grab the woman's matter in my hand?

JOHN: No. This. The matter in hand. This situation. The young woman down there. We need to do something.

MATTHEW: Where is the doctor?

JOHN: He disappeared.

MATTHEW: Where?

JOHN: I don't know.

MATTHEW: He needs to tell us what to do.

JOHN: He is not quite in a state to do that. And we know what to do.

MATTHEW: Do we?

JOHN: Yes. We get her out of there however we can.

MATTHEW: Yes. Of course that's what we need to do. How?

STELLA steps forward.

STELLA: Where is the young woman?

MATTHEW: Young woman?

STELLA: Where is she? May?

MATTHEW: May you what?

STELLA: The young girl. She's not here.

74

MATTHEW: Is she not?

STELLA: No. What have you done with her?

MATTHEW: I have done nothing.

There is banging.

STELLA: What is that?

MATTHEW: Nothing.

JOHN: Come on, let's get you back.

STELLA: No. What was it?

MATTHEW: It was nothing.

DR MAYNARD enters.

DR MAYNARD: Gentlemen.

MATTHEW: Ah, Governor.

DR MAYNARD: How are you?

MATTHEW: I think you'll find I'm tip top, healthy to burst out of my skin.

DR MAYNARD: You sound positively happy.

MATTHEW: Not suspiciously so?

DR MAYNARD: (*Suspicious.*) Not suspicious, no.

MATTHEW: Good. Good. So. How do you find being a Governor?

DR MAYNARD: Interesting. Here. (*Hands out a copy of his book.*).

MATTHEW: Is this for me to read?

DR MAYNARD: I can't imagine what else you might do with it.

MATTHEW: Sneeze into it. Use it as a pillow. Line my breeches in case I'm beaten. (*Laughs.*).

DR MAYNARD: Are you all right?

MATTHEW: Fine. Absolutely fine. Better than fine. What is this?

DR MAYNARD: My writings.

MATTHEW: Upon what?

DR MAYNARD: Upon madness.

MATTHEW: Is there much to say?

The banging again. DR MAYNARD looks around.

DR MAYNARD: What is that?

MATTHEW: I heard nothing. John?

JOHN: Nothing.

MATTHEW: You were going to tell us what's in your writings.

DR MAYNARD: My thoughts upon the treatment of London's mad.
Is your father here? I requested some time with your painter and your father appeared happy with the arrangement. I wondered if perhaps I could see him now.

The banging begins again.

There it is again. What is it?

MATTHEW begins tapping his foot.

MATTHEW: It is me.

OLIVER shouts.

MATTHEW shouts too, attempting to cover up the sound.

DR MAYNARD: Why are you shouting?

JOHN: He's shouting for his father.

MATTHEW: I am. (*Shouts.*) Doctor. Father. Daddy.

JOHN: But he doesn't know where he is.

MATTHEW: No.

Faint singing.

DR MAYNARD: Who is that?

MATTHEW: There are always voices here.

STELLA: Excuse me.

MATTHEW: The doctor is busy.

DR MAYNARD: The patient may speak.

MATTHEW: She is a bore, Governor. You do not have to listen.

DR MAYNARD: I want to. Go on.

STELLA: They have lost a patient.

MATTHEW: Lost a patient?

MATTHEW laughs too much.

Lost a patient. Lost a patient.

STELLA: The young girl from the farm. She was with me and she has gone and they won't say where she is.

DR MAYNARD: So where is she?

A scream.

MATTHEW screams.

DR CAREW enters, bedraggled.

DR CAREW: Ah, a gaggle of doctors. No, a case of doctors. A medicine chest of doctors.

DR MAYNARD: Doctor. I arranged to come and see your patient.

DR CAREW: Patient?

DR MAYNARD: The painter.

DR CAREW looks at MATTHEW.

DR CAREW shakes his ears, tries to get something out of them.

DR CAREW: Can't hear a thing. Full of ear wigs. Blighty things crawled in while I was asleep. No. Can't hear.

DR MAYNARD: What is happening?

DR CAREW: What do you mean?

DR MAYNARD: You heard me then.

DR CAREW: I didn't.

DR MAYNARD: You heard that.

DR CAREW: I didn't.

DR MAYNARD: Where is the painter?

Banging. MATTHEW starts dancing again. Screaming. MATTHEW screams. Singing. JOHN sings too. They stop.

STELLA: Is she down there with him?

DR CAREW: Her mind is scrambled. The words make no sense.

STELLA: I do make sense.

DR CAREW: I have earwigs in my ears. I can not hear a thing.

DR MAYNARD: Then perhaps your son should take you off and help evacuate your ears.

DR CAREW: I think not.

DR MAYNARD: So you do hear me again?

DR CAREW: The earwig was turning around.

DR MAYNARD: Matthew, take your father and get him something for his ears.

MATTHEW: Yes, sir.

DR MAYNARD: I will see to this patient.

MATTHEW: Yes, sir.

DR MAYNARD: Go on.

MATTHEW begins to walk. The banging starts and he tries to get his walk in time with the noise.

DR MAYNARD: *(To JOHN.)* What is happening?

JOHN: Dr Carew had a late night, sir.

DR MAYNARD: And this girl, is she missing?

JOHN: I don't know.

DR MAYNARD: And the painter?

JOHN: I believe he has been moved, sir. Temporarily.

DR MAYNARD: Then you will show me where he is?

JOHN: I suppose so, sir.

DR MAYNARD: And then perhaps you can find the missing patient.

STELLA: Thank you, doctor.

JOHN leaves. DR MAYNARD follows.

STELLA looks around, then goes to leave. As she does, the trapdoor slowly opens.

SCENE TWO

The trapdoor opens and OLIVER looks around. He sees it is clear, and brings up MAY, then goes back down. MAY is alone. She stares out.

MAY: Look at your faces. All of you looking at me.
The wind blows and my skin is cold. Are you cold? Do you listen to me?
I do not belong here.
I am tired.
Stand still. I can not see you. You move and I don't know where I am.

Laughs.

OLIVER emerges from the trapdoor. He carries a canvas and his paints. He sets up.

You left me on my own.
Have you come to take me home?

OLIVER: No.

OLIVER gets a chair, positions it.

Sit there.

MAY sits.

Put this on.

OLIVER gives MAY a top hat and she puts it on.

You have to cover your hair.

OLIVER begins to paint, occasionally picking up a knife which he sharpens on a whetstone.

Stay still. I said still.

MAY: They're watching me.

OLIVER: There's no-one here.

MAY: The wind blows me.

OLIVER: There's no wind.

MAY: I need to go to the pigs.

OLIVER: The doors are locked.

MAY: You're painting. What are you painting?

OLIVER: I am painting you.

MAY: Why are you painting me?

OLIVER: So I can look at you. I'm trying to paint you and not think about doing anything else.
Are you hungry? No. I didn't say that.
I am painting you.

MAY: I'm ready to go now.

OLIVER: Stay there.

  I like the smell of you. Stay still.

  MAY stands up. OLIVER pushes her back.

  Stay still. Blood smells dark. Do you like the smell of blood? No.

  MAY sits still.

MAY: The floor's burning my feet.

  MAY lifts her feet.

  It hurts.

OLIVER: How do you kill the pigs? Do you cut their throats? The blood is hot.

MAY: I can hear the birds. Do you hear them?

OLIVER: No.

MAY: They're talking.

  MAY laughs.

  They're talking about me. *(Listens.)* How do they know all that?

  OLIVER stands. Walks around, goes back to the painting, walks around. He is restless, driven. He touches her hair, stands close to her.

OLIVER: My sister had hair like this. I told her to sit like you are. I painted her.

  OLIVER pulls back, takes a breath.

  It didn't happen until I had finished with her.

  There is a banging on the door. MAY moves towards it.

  Leave it.

MAY obeys.

JOHN creeps in. OLIVER sees and grabs MAY.

Don't come any closer.
Get back.

JOHN shrinks back.

We see DR MAYNARD appear above, then NANCY. They watch.

MAY: The birds are talking about you. They're watching you.

MAY laughs.

OLIVER: Stop that. Don't laugh.
There is banging again.
Who is it?

We hear SAMUEL's voice.

SAMUEL: Let me in.

OLIVER: No.

OLIVER walks around MAY.

Do the pigs scream when they are killed?

MAY: They cry like babies.

OLIVER: I was a baby once. My mother said I cried a lot. She
said my sister cried too. We used to play. My sister played
with me.

We hear JOHN's voice.

JOHN: We won't hurt you. Let us in.
Come on. Let us in.

OLIVER puts his hands over his ears.

OLIVER: *(Cries out.)* No.

*OLIVER goes back to the painting. He grabs the brush and paints
furiously.*

They're scared of me. They don't know. No-one knows.

There is more banging at the door.

(Shouts.) Go away.

The trapdoor above them opens quietly and NANCY is lowered down carrying a tray of meat, and stops above OLIVER.

OLIVER grabs MAY and retreats into the dark corner, then he smells and slowly comes out as NANCY dangles.

NANCY: For what we are about to receive may the Lord make us truly grateful.

As OLIVER goes to grab her, NANCY is pulled up away from him and he is stormed from behind by JOHN, SAL, RICHARD, SAMUEL and MATTHEW. His hat comes off.

OLIVER: No. No.

MAY rushes towards MATTHEW.

MAY: That's my Billy.

RICHARD and SAMUEL stop her.

SAL: Take her back.

MAY is dragged off.

JOHN and SAL lock OLIVER into restraints.

OLIVER: Don't. Don't chain me. My hat. They're in my hair.

DR CAREW strides on, followed by DR MAYNARD and ANNABEL.

DR MAYNARD sees OLIVER, places his hat on his head.

DR CAREW: You have him?

JOHN: Yes, Doctor.

DR CAREW: Put extra chains on him.

DR MAYNARD: Is that necessary?

DR CAREW: Indeed.

OLIVER: Sir, help me.

DR MAYNARD: I think he will be fine.

OLIVER: I wasn't going to hurt her. I loved my sister. They said I had to do it then they stared at me for doing it. They came through my hair. They'll come through yours.

OLIVER is approached with extra chains.

I was only going to paint her.

DR CAREW: *(Laughs.)* With your tongue and teeth? Tighten his chains.

OLIVER cries, panics.

OLIVER: Don't. Please. I wasn't going to hurt her. I wasn't. Please don't.

DR CAREW: Put him in the dark.

OLIVER: *(Cries out.)* No.

DR MAYNARD: He could be found an alternate place. Somewhere he can paint and not be watched.

DR CAREW: He's a draw for the crowds. The crowd brings money. Go on. Take him.

OLIVER: No. No.

OLIVER is taken down into the cellar.

DR CAREW: Right, come along. No time to shilly shally. Move. Come on, come on, man.

SAMUEL enters and assembles his desk.

DR CAREW: Now patients to see. Who have we?

SAMUEL: Only myself, sir.

DR CAREW: But you do not care to leave.

SAMUEL: No.

DR MAYNARD: I am sure you might.

SAMUEL: No, sir.

DR CAREW: Next. Next.

JOHN brings forward STELLA.

SAMUEL: Stella Mornington.

DR CAREW: What do you have to say?

STELLA: Thank you for seeing me, Doctor. Has the gentleman poet Laurence spoken to you?

DR CAREW: Poet? What poet?

ANNABEL: Actually I asked for you to be seen.

STELLA: Not the poet?

ANNABEL: No.

DR CAREW: What are you talking about?

DR MAYNARD: Do we know anything about this woman's case, Samuel?

SAMUEL: *(Reads.)* "Stella Mornington was admitted by her husband after the birth of a child. She displayed erratic and violent behaviour."

DR CAREW: Matthew, we have heard nothing from you. What do you see?

MATTHEW: A patient.

DR CAREW: But what can we learn from it?

MATTHEW: You told me, sir, we learn nothing from these lunatics.

DR CAREW: I never spoke those words. I have been singing, yes, and playing music.

DR MAYNARD: What music?

DR CAREW: I didn't say music.

DR MAYNARD: Are you all right?

DR CAREW: All right? I am more than all right.

STELLA: May I speak?

DR MAYNARD: Yes.

DR CAREW: He allows the lunatic to speak. God help us all. Go on. Have the floor. We are your audience. Go on.

STELLA: I would like to thank the lady here for raising my case.

DR CAREW: The lady? (*Laughs.*) The language of society.

DR MAYNARD: Allow her to speak.

DR CAREW: You challenge me again. Governor, I am in my rights to ask you to leave. My head is hot and you are hurting it and please stand back.

ANNABEL: Would you like to continue?

STELLA: I know that when I was admitted, my reason was gone from me and I was unable to control my actions or my speech. My madness was exacerbated by the fact that my child was taken from me and placed I don't know where. However, in the time I have been here, my reason has slowly returned and I find myself a rational human being.

DR CAREW: Yes, yes. Get to it.

ANNABEL: Husband. *(To STELLA.)* Continue.

STELLA: And so I ask that I be allowed to leave.

DR MAYNARD: And you consider yourself cured?

STELLA: Indeed.

DR CAREW: Cured? Ha. A mad doctor allows his patients to judge whether or not they are mad. Why not ask a whore whether she is clean and free of disease.

ANNABEL: Doctor.

DR CAREW: The woman is clearly mad. If she can speak that clearly and argue that reasonably then she has no business being on the outside world. Imagine the damage she would wrought.

DR MAYNARD: Matthew?

MATTHEW: What?

DR MAYNARD: This woman before you. How does she present herself?

MATTHEW: Her hair is a little unruly.

DR MAYNARD: No. Does she make sense? Does she reason well?

MATTHEW: I think so.

DR MAYNARD: Then she should be discharged.

DR CAREW: All right. Discharge her.

STELLA: Thank you.
Before I go, I do have something more to say.
I do not deny that there have been small acts of kindness, yet you allowed the public to jeer and taunt. When I felt as though I wanted never to be seen, I looked up to see face upon face staring at me as though my condition could illuminate something for the viewer. Yet my condition illuminated nothing. We are all in the dark in this building. I wish, sirs, you would consider what effect it has.

DR CAREW: But you are cured.

STELLA: I may be cured, sir, but I am humiliated and have nowhere to go, for my husband no longer requires my presence.

ANNABEL: You can come with me. I'll help you make some arrangements.

DR CAREW: Wife. You step over the threshold.

ANNABEL: I do not care. Come.

ANNABEL and STELLA leave.

DR CAREW: What a pair of chicken-breasted wagtails. Any more patients?

SAMUEL: No. All done.

DR CAREW: Good. Well, Governor, you can go now.

DR MAYNARD: I thought I would check the patients.

DR CAREW: There is no need. I will do that.

DR MAYNARD: You said I could speak to some of them.

DR CAREW: I don't remember that.

DR MAYNARD: We spoke of it.

DR CAREW: We don't speak of it now. Good day, Governor.

DR MAYNARD: If that is your wish. Good day.

DR MAYNARD leaves. SAMUEL packs up his books.

DR CAREW: Samuel.

SAMUEL: You're not going to make me leave?

DR CAREW: No.

SAMUEL: Sir, are you all right?

DR CAREW: No.
What now do I do?

SAMUEL: What do you mean?

DR CAREW: I don't know.

DR CAREW feels his head.

My head is cool as my brain. A brain is a cold and vicious object and if heated it becomes liquid.

SAMUEL: I don't understand.

DR CAREW: Understand? What? Where is my wife? Wife. Where are you?

SAMUEL: She has gone with the lady, sir.

DR CAREW: I tire of this.
You have all been discharged and I have to stay? Where are you? Wife? She doesn't come.

SAMUEL: She can't hear you.

DR CAREW: Where is my dirty oyster then. My she-dog. My gin swiller. My concoctor of spells.
Penny a drink and get your kill-grief, your heart's ease here. Drown our sorrows. Awash me with liquor and take me with you, for I tire of this.
I have not been well.
I have not been well.

SAMUEL: Come, sir. Come.

SAMUEL helps DR CAREW off.

SCENE THREE

The grotto. The BEDLAMITES play. GARDENIA hands them money and they move on. LAURENCE creeps up behind and clamps his hands over GARDENIA's eyes.

LAURENCE: Are you happy to see me?

GARDENIA: My dear friend, of course I am.

LAURENCE: How very touching.

GARDENIA: My very brilliant and dear friend.

LAURENCE: Even more touching.

GARDENIA: How flow the precious words?

LAURENCE: They come. The muse occasionally does her thing.

GARDENIA: I'm sure it's all shot with gold.

LAURENCE: I have some moments of brilliance.

GARDENIA: Of course you do.

LAURENCE: You asked to meet.

GARDENIA: Do I have to give a reason?

LAURENCE: I suppose not. I do not have much time.

GARDENIA: Are you on your way to somewhere?

LAURENCE: Someone.

GARDENIA: The mad girl still? At this hour? It's not a visiting day.

LAURENCE: I know. Thank you.

GARDENIA: You really do persist.

LAURENCE: It is not persistence. It is love. She will be mine. I will have her.

GARDENIA: Then she is a lucky girl.

LAURENCE: You change your view?

GARDENIA: I wish you happiness.

LAURENCE: Thank you.

GARDENIA: One small thing. Last time we met, you gave me your word.

LAURENCE: Did I?

GARDENIA: Yes. You gave your word and said you would act upon it.

LAURENCE: It doesn't spring into my mind.

GARDENIA: You said you would see to the situation of the woman in Bedlam.

LAURENCE: Did I?

GARDENIA: Yes. Have you done anything? She must be rotting there.

LAURENCE: I have been singularly busy.

GARDENIA: You did give your word.

LAURENCE: Maybe.

GARDENIA: You did. A word is a word.

LAURENCE: And pedantry is pedantry.

GARDENIA: Is that what it is?

LAURENCE: Gardenia, you will never remarry if you continue to question men in this way.

GARDENIA: I am so sorry.

LAURENCE: You stand there questioning me, instead of asking me how I am.

GARDENIA: Nor have you asked me how I am.

LAURENCE: I can see you are fine.

GARDENIA: And I can see you are.

STELLA enters, transformed. GARDENIA sees her.

I did ask you here for a reason. I have someone to see you.

LAURENCE: Have you sprung my love from that place? Gardenia!

LAURENCE turns, sees it is STELLA.

Stella!
This is not funny.

GARDENIA: It was not my intention to be funny. I thought you could explain why you did nothing to help her.

LAURENCE: I was going to.

GARDENIA: Don't lie. Have you nothing to say to her?

LAURENCE: No. Nothing.

GARDENIA: I thought you might appreciate the opportunity to apologise.

LAURENCE: I have nothing to apologise for. I have to leave.

STELLA: Laurence.

LAURENCE: I am late.

GARDENIA tries to block him. LAURENCE pushes her.

GARDENIA: Do not go.

LAURENCE: Why should I stay? To listen to the two of you admonishing me for my very own nature, for which I am hardly responsible?

GARDENIA: Do you not want to know of your child?

LAURENCE: Madam, I have other things that are more worthy of my time.

LAURENCE leaves.

GARDENIA: That was incredibly stupid of me.

STELLA: I expected nothing more of him.

GARDENIA: I don't know what I hoped for. How naïve.

STELLA: It is not naïve. Just misplaced. Thank you for trying, but he is not capable of change.

GARDENIA: I suppose he is a habitual creature. What did he always say?

Whereon I think of you my love, my sweet,
It is ne'er too long before we two friends meet.

STELLA: *Before we two lovers meet.*

GARDENIA: And his fatuous thing, about how boring happiness was.

STELLA: All happiness is the same,

They speak together:

Like boiled oats.

STELLA: Well, I think I showed him real misery and yet he wouldn't stay and partake in it.

GARDENIA: And I made him suffer with my own cheerful disposition.

STELLA: Good.

GARDENIA: What to do now? He's gone to see the poor girl.

STELLA: There's nothing he can do before tomorrow. They won't let him in.

GARDENIA: I suppose not.

STELLA: Gardenia. I want to thank you.

GARDENIA: Please don't.

STELLA: But I do.

GARDENIA: I won't hear a thing. You owe me nothing.

ANNABEL enters behind STELLA. She carries the child.

STELLA: But I want to apologise that you had to look upon me in my previous state. I do not care to think of myself in that condition.

GARDENIA: You are not to apologise. You are how I see you now. I have no memory of you then.

STELLA: That's very kind.

ANNABEL brings the child to STELLA for a reunion. GARDENIA and ANNABEL watch for a moment.

STELLA: Thank you. Thank you.

ANNABEL and STELLA leave.

STELLA remains behind with the child.

SCENE FOUR

Bedlam. Night. SAL arrives and removes her coat. She tidies and sweeps. She and JOHN start locking up cells and checking on patients. RICHARD emerges.

RICHARD: Dark night. Moon's full.

SAL: Be a busy night, then.
Take this.

SAL passes him the broom.

Finish up.

RICHARD sweeps. He turns and watches SAL as she locks up patients.

RICHARD: Sal.

SAL: No.

RICHARD: You don't know what I was gonna ask.

SAL: I do.

RICHARD: A quick one. That's all I ask for. A yank on the old bell rope. A squeeze of the udder.

SAL: Get in.

SAL pushes him in his cell, turns to JOHN.

Where's the wife?

JOHN: Won't be back till dawn.

SAL: You can go and have a sleep if you like.

JOHN: You sure?

SAL: I ain't saying it twice.

JOHN leaves.

It is all quiet.

SAL checks it's clear, then takes MAY out of her cell and places her to the side of the stage.

She hears a noise and goes off, comes back quietly with LAURENCE.

LAURENCE: I cannot see.

SAL: Shh. It's night.

LAURENCE: I am not stupid, woman.

SAL: Are you not, sir?

LAURENCE: If you want this (*Holds up money.*), I would advise you to show some respect.

SAL: If you want to stay here, I would cross my palm.

LAURENCE hands over money and SAL checks it.

LAURENCE: You do not trust me.

SAL: I do not trust anyone, sir.

LAURENCE: I am a gentleman.

SAL: I am sure you are.
You can stay till the first cock crows.

LAURENCE: And no-one will know?

SAL: There's no-one to know.

LAURENCE: I have never felt love like this.

SAL: I don't want to hear about love.
You've given me the money. First cock, I said, and you're out.

LAURENCE: I'll be ready.

SAL: Stay there.

SAL silences LAURENCE and gets MAY, brings her to him, then leaves.

LAURENCE looks at MAY.

LAURENCE: Hello.

LAURENCE gets out his scroll and unravels a poem. He clears his throat. He speaks slowly, carefully, enunciating every syllable.

I am a poet.
I write poems.
I say that because that is what poets do.
Can you hear me? It's slightly disconcerting. Nod if you can hear me.
I have come to visit you to talk. So far you have not spoken to me. I thought instead I should read you something that I wrote.

Clears his throat again, turns to the moon.

Moon, illuminate my words and bathe them in your silver glow.

My love, a girl, so young, fresh born from soil,
My love for her will make me sweat and toil.

MAY turns away.

I fear you find it dull.
Speak.
May?
Do not ignore me.

MAY: Where am I?

LAURENCE: Ah! You speak.

MAY goes to run off. LAURENCE grabs her.

LAURENCE: Stay.
Listen to me.

LAURENCE reads from a poem. MAY tries to walk away and he holds onto her, follows her round in circles.

The eye did sweep the room and then with grace,
It landed not on her but a new, untouched face.

MAY stops.

You like it?

MAY snatches the paper from his hands and screws it up.

You don't like it.

MAY grabs his arms.

What is it, my love?

MAY: I have lapped from the lakes of ducks.

LAURENCE: I think that not a wise idea. The water could be diseased.

MAY: I have eaten from the bowls of dogs.

LAURENCE: I wish you wouldn't. I could bring you a bowl.

MAY turns to him suddenly.

MAY: I have to go.

LAURENCE: You can't go. We are locked in, you see.

MAY moves away. She holds her head.

MAY: There is the heat of a fire in here and I have ash for brains.

LAURENCE: My love.

MAY tears off a piece of the paper and begins to eat it.

That's the only copy.

LAURENCE snatches the poem.

I love you and I will do anything for you but you can not eat my work.

MAY walks away.

Stop.

MAY lies down.

Don't sleep. Dear sweet May, the bud of my hedge, the blossom of my longing.

MAY wakes, gets up.

MAY: I hear the waves.

LAURENCE: My love.

MAY: Where are you?

LAURENCE: I am here.
 May. Look at me.

MAY looks at him.

We see BILLY, who is breaking into the building, scaling walls and climbing roofs.

MAY: Where is Billy?

LAURENCE: Not that again.

MAY: I want Billy.

LAURENCE: I know you do. All right. (*Puts on rural accent.*) I am Billy.

MAY: You are here?

LAURENCE: I am back from the sea.

MAY: You have come for me.

LAURENCE: Course I have. Come here.

LAURENCE pulls her towards him and puts his arms around her.

Kiss me.

LAURENCE kisses her.

MAY begins to scream.

MAY: You're not Billy.

LAURENCE: Don't scream. They'll hear us.

MAY: Billy. Billy.

LAURENCE grabs her and puts a hand over her mouth.

LAURENCE: If you scream I'll get caught. You understand?

MAY nods.

You won't make a sound?

MAY shakes her head. LAURENCE takes his hand off.

We see BILLY still clambering over roofs and breaking his way into the building.

MAY: Who are you?

LAURENCE: I am a poet.

MAY: Is it night?

LAURENCE: Yes.

MAY: How is the moon?

LAURENCE: The moon is white. It glows in the dark sky like a lamp.

MAY: It is white of bone.

LAURENCE: May.

MAY: I move it. When I breathe it travels across the black sky. If I stop breathing it stays still, among the stars.

LAURENCE: I love you.

MAY: I love Billy. I love him as the moon rises and falls. As the leaves unfurl and curl and die.
I love his breath and his beating heart.

LAURENCE puts his hand on her leg, raises her skirts.

What are you doing?

LAURENCE: You know what I am doing.

MAY: No.
Get off.

LAURENCE: Don't pretend.
Come on.

MAY: No. Don't.
No.

LAURENCE pushes MAY to the floor and climbs on her. She screams but he continues to attack her, then they fight and he hits her. She screams again.

NANCY emerges and begins to shout.

NANCY: Help. Help. Help.

BILLY appears and pulls LAURENCE off, hits him. They fight and SAL, RICHARD and SAMUEL rush out.

BILLY hits LAURENCE, who passes out. BILLY is restrained.

BILLY: I'll kill him.

SAL: Grab him.

BILLY: Let me get him.

SAL: Hold him.

BILLY: May. Are you all right?

MAY: Who are you?

BILLY: Billy.

MATTHEW enters. MAY sees him.

MAY: You ain't Billy.
Here is my Billy come back to me.

MAY rushes towards him. MATTHEW backs off.

Oh, Billy. I have been in the dark. Kiss me.

BILLY: Let me go. May. I am Billy.

BILLY breaks free, rushes forward, goes to hit MATTHEW.

BILLY: Get away from her.

SAL stops him.

SAL: Get your salt ridden arse out of here.

BILLY: I ain't going nowhere.

RICHARD: You better had. They're coming.

BILLY: I'm staying here.

RICHARD: Then you better hide.

BILLY runs off, grabs some clothes, dresses as a female patient.

SAL: *(To MATTHEW.)* Don't say nothing.

MATTHEW: Nothing.

SAL: No. Nothing.

SAL tries to revive LAURENCE.

You got to go, sir. Sir.

SAL slaps him. LAURENCE comes round.

LAURENCE: I am not leaving without her.

LAURENCE stands, pushes SAL out of the way.

SAL: Get out.

LAURENCE: No.

The first cockerel sounds.

SAL: The first cock. You said.

LAURENCE: Where's that yokel?

SAL: Hide. Quick.

LAURENCE runs, hides as JOHN enters. They pretend nothing has happened.

JOHN: Sir.

MATTHEW: Good morning.

JOHN: You're here early.

MATTHEW: I like to keep them on their toes.

JOHN: Quiet night?

SAL: Quiet as death.

MATTHEW: These people are just going back to their beds.

NANCY: They're not. There was a man here.

SAL: She always says that.

NANCY: But there was. He's here still.

RICHARD: He was one of her gentlemen. She reckons she's still on her back.

NANCY: I'm a clean girl, a good girl.
The man is in here.

SAL: Where would he be then?

SAL fakes looking for him.

Hello. Hello. Can't see no-one.
Come on. Back to your cells.

NANCY stands still.

NANCY: The Lord watches you.

SAL: He's watching you and all. He wants you back in your cell.

MATTHEW: I'll take her.

NANCY: There is a star above your head. Look. You have been marked out.

MATTHEW: *(To JOHN.)* You hear that?

JOHN: I did.

NANCY: The Lord wishes that you take me to my straw.

MATTHEW: The Lord wishes that?

NANCY: The Lord himself.

NANCY leaves with MATTHEW. JOHN stops him.

JOHN: Come on. Get back. Too early in the day for standing around.

JOHN shepherds SAMUEL and RICHARD back to their cells.

JOHN and SAL remain.

So you had a quiet night?

SAL: Yep.

JOHN: Sun's coming up.

SAL: Looks like it.

JOHN: Another day.

SAL: Yep.

JOHN passes SAL a broom.

JOHN: You gonna stand there all day?

SAL: No. Are you?

JOHN: No.

JOHN takes another broom.

Who was the man she talked about?

SAL: What?

JOHN: She said there was some man hiding here.

SAL: (*Laughs.*) You been here too long. You been here forever, ain't you? You started listening to them. You must be catching it, what they got.

They sweep. SAL stops.

That's the thing, ain't it? They get to leave if they get better, but we poor sods don't.

They begin cleaning, preparing for the open day.

SCENE FIVE

Bedlam. Open day. The BEDLAMITES play and a queue forms.

PHYLLIS, drunk, sings with NARRATOR:

Into a pond stark nak'd I ran,
And cast away my clothes, sir,
Without the help of any man,
Made shift to run away, sir.

How I got out I have forgot,
I do not well remember;
Or whether it was cold or hot,
In June or in December.
Tom Bedlam's but a sage to me,
I speak in sober sadness,
For more strange visions do I see
Than he in all his madness.

Do you not see my love of late,
Like Titan in her glory?
Did you not know she was my mate,
And I must write her story.

My silken suits do now decay,
My cups of gold are vanished,
And all my friends do wear away,
As I from them were banished.

My silver cups are turned to earth,
I'm jeered by every clown;
I was a better man by birth,
Till fortune cast me down.

To picking straws now must I go,
My time in Bedlam spending.
Good folks you your beginning know,
But do not know your ending.

NARRATOR: When in the future you meet us Tom O'Bedlams,
think on us. I may be filthy, reeking of the street. I may
talk to myself, my clothes be peeling themselves off my
skin.
But if we meet one day, I want you think on this.
Think what embroidered waistcoat once embraced my
chest.
What perfumed breath once crept out of my mouth. What
soft hands I once used to hold my children.

I have said enough.
Enough. Enough.

SAMUEL sets up his table and books.

*DR CAREW enters shouting, ANNABEL with him, PHYLLIS following
drunkenly. JOHN and MATTHEW also follow.*

ANNABEL: Doctor. Please. Listen to me.

DR CAREW: Listen to you? Why?

ANNABEL: What have you been drinking?

DR CAREW: Nothing.

ANNABEL: Doctor?

DR CAREW: Nothing.

ANNABEL: I am not stupid.

DR CAREW: Are you sure?

PHYLLIS: The doctor is fine.

ANNABEL: Matthew. Get rid of this woman.

DR CAREW: No.

ANNABEL: I can smell it on you.

DR CAREW: Watch. I can walk as straight a line as anyone.

DR CAREW attempts to walk in a straight line.

My son keeps moving the floor.

MATTHEW: No sir.

DR CAREW: I may have had one drink.

ANNABEL: More than one.

DR CAREW: Two.

ANNABEL: More than two. You are drunk.

DR CAREW: Drunk, madam?

ANNABEL: Yes. Drunk.

DR CAREW: (*Laughs.*) I may have been bit by a barn mouse, I may have loaded my cart, killed my dog, got corns in my head, been to Jericho, been at the Geneva, seen a flock of moons, lost my rudder, been to the salt water, been in the bibbing plot, drunk more than I bled.
I may be staggerish, stewed, pidgeon-eyed, nimptopsical, in my attitudes, cherry merry, muddy, borachio, foxed, wet in both eyes, tipsy, brandy-faced, chirping merry, smelling of onions, pie-eyed, as dizzy as a goose, woozy, bladdered, trammelled, piss-maker and swill tub.
But drunk, no madam. Not drunk.

PHYLLIS: Have a drink.

PHYLLIS falls over and lies on the floor, drunkenly.

ANNABEL: This can not continue.

DR CAREW: Oh, don't be such a bore. I am English and it's what we do. We are a nation of pale-skinned fighting

drunkards, and always will be.
Let me to my patients. John.

JOHN: It is not a Saturday, sir. It is open day. Visiting day. The day that people come and view the patients.

DR CAREW: I know what day it is.
Where is the beauty? Fetch her here. I need something to look at. Come on. Get her.

JOHN gets MAY.

ANNABEL: What are you are doing, sir?

DR CAREW: I am seeing my patients.

ANNABEL: For entertainment?

DR CAREW: Why else would I see them? I can't take their madness away.

MAY is brought to DR CAREW.

Aha. How is my beauty?

MAY: Waiting for the world to stop moving and the waves to still. Waiting for my Billy to step from his boat.

MAY calls out.

Billy. Billy. I need Billy.

BILLY rushes out, still dressed as a woman.

BILLY: I am here.

DR CAREW: You are not Billy.

MAY: You are not Billy.

RICHARD: Who is that?

MAY: It is a milkmaid from the farm.

BILLY: I came to rescue her from the poet.

DR CAREW: Poet? What damned poet?

BILLY: The one who was locked in with her.

DR CAREW: You talk nonsense. She is mad. Lock her away.

BILLY: No. I come to see May.

RICHARD: Look at her bubbies. Let me touch her.

DR CAREW: I have touched many a woman. Go on, help yourself.

RICHARD grabs BILLY.

BILLY: Get off me.

RICHARD: I love this one. I don't just want her to pull my sugar stick. I want this one for ever. To hold and to marry and to breed with. She is so beautiful. I love you.

BILLY: Get off.

RICHARD: The more you protest, the more I will love you.

RICHARD starts chasing BILLY, who chases MAY.

BILLY: May.

MAY: Go away.

RICHARD: Come here.

ANNABEL: Stop them.

SAL runs after them and floors RICHARD.

DR CAREW: (*Shouts.*) Stop. Stop. Stop.

ANNABEL: Matthew. Husband.

DR CAREW: Did I hear a shrew? A-squeaking and a-wailing?

ANNABEL: You are not fit to doctor.

DR CAREW: Fit? I am the fittest man alive.

DR CAREW sees BILLY.

Who is this woman?
Where is my she-dog?

DR CAREW pinches PHYLLIS' bottom. She squeals.

Get me a drink. Let us begin the day with a jolt.

ANNABEL: Stop.
You have to stop now. You are not well.

DR CAREW: I am as well as any man. Let us have booze.
Booze, lovely booze.

PHYLLIS: Fill your boots here. Heart's ease. Kick in the guts.

ANNABEL: *(To JOHN.)* Stop. Please stop her.

PHYLLIS runs, JOHN chases her.

DR MAYNARD enters.

RICHARD and SAL leave quietly.

DR MAYNARD: Doctor.

ANNABEL: Thank the Lord.

DR MAYNARD: What is happening?

DR CAREW: Wife, darling, doctor darling.

ANNABEL: He is ill, doctor. Please.

DR CAREW: "He is ill, doctor."

DR CAREW goes to leave.

DR MAYNARD: Where do you go?

DR CAREW: To sport myself.

DR MAYNARD restrains him.

(Bellows.) Let me go.

ANNABEL: Do not let him go.

DR CAREW: Shut this stupid woman up.

DR MAYNARD: Stop it. You are not well, sir.

DR CAREW: Let me assure you, my mind is fastly tightened within my bone dome.

DR CAREW begins to pace. He circles, restless, occasionally laughing, talking under his breath.

My mind is a fine thing. A fine thing. A mind is a good thing.

ANNABEL follows him.

ANNABEL: Stop. Please stop.

DR CAREW opens his flies.

ANNABEL screams and runs, chased by CAREW.

Get off.

DR CAREW: Come for a quiffing, madam.

MATTHEW tries to stop him.

DR CAREW laughs.

Here. Have some money. I have too much money. Let me buy you a house. A horse. A stallion. Come here. Let me see your dark cave. Your cracks.

DR MAYNARD: Get him.

MATTHEW and DR MAYNARD grab DR CAREW.

Sir, tell me what day of the week it is.

DR CAREW: Do not make me walk in a line.

DR MAYNARD: Who am I?

CAREW laughs.

DR CAREW: You do not know?

DR MAYNARD: How many fingers can you see?

DR CAREW: I am not in danger of losing my sight.

DR MAYNARD: Who is the woman here?

DR CAREW: Is there a woman?

DR MAYNARD: There is.

DR CAREW: I thought it merely a chair.

DR CAREW weeps.

Oh, I have been ill and I am tired.

DR MAYNARD: You weep.

DR CAREW: The more you cry the less you piss.

ANNABEL: I fear, doctor, I am at the end of my tether.

DR MAYNARD: Sir, come with me.

DR MAYNARD leads CAREW away.

Let me see.
Come on, doctor.

DR CAREW drops his trousers and DR MAYNARD inspects him.

You have lesions.

DR CAREW: They are not lesions. The rats have nibbled me,
sir. They asked to come under the covers and what was I to
say? They were shivering.

DR MAYNARD returns.

ANNABEL: What are we to do?

DR MAYNARD: Take your father aside.

MATTHEW: Yes, doctor.

DR CAREW: I have no need of a side. I am chasing special
ideas. The make up of the brain is cold jelly.

DR MAYNARD waits until he has gone.

DR MAYNARD: Madam, I am afraid it appears Doctor Carew is infected with the gentleman's disease.
He will need treatment but he has left it far too long.

ANNABEL: He should be treated in his own hospital.

DR MAYNARD: You want him to be admitted here?

ANNABEL: He argues it is the best place for the mad to be treated. He is mad?

DR MAYNARD: He has mania.

ANNABEL: Then he can come here.

DR MAYNARD: Of course, there are implications. By that I mean. Well, you will also need to see a doctor.

ANNABEL: The most we have shared for many years is a nod across the breakfast table. Other women will need the treatment, but not me.

DR MAYNARD: Samuel.

DR MAYNARD dictates and SAMUEL writes.

"Dr Carew has mania as a result of the gentleman's disease, and requires treatment with mercury and solitude and calm in order for his equilibrium to return."

DR CAREW overhears.

DR CAREW: Do you say I am mad?

DR MAYNARD: Yes, doctor.

DR CAREW: Mad? I am a mad doctor, not a mad doctor.

DR MAYNARD: John, we will have to admit him.

JOHN: You want me to admit the doctor?

DR MAYNARD: Yes.

PHYLLIS: Is he ill?

SAL steps forward.

DR CAREW: What are you doing? Don't touch me.

DR MAYNARD: It is all right, sir. You are among kind hands.

JOHN searches his pockets. DR MAYNARD helps. They remove keys, money, a purse, and hand them to ANNABEL.

DR CAREW: What do you do to me? Your hands are soiled. I am fragile. Do not touch me.

DR MAYNARD: Hold him.

They undress him.

DR CAREW: Do not take my coat. I am unravelling. Allow me my clothes. My skin is naked. I pimple like a goose.
I start like a deer. I make like a bird at night.
Madam do not do this to me.
I said do not do this.
Maynard?

DR MAYNARD: Yes.

DR CAREW: You think me ill.

DR MAYNARD: I am afraid so.

DR CAREW: And you intend to lock me up?
Look at me. I said look me in the eye.

DR MAYNARD: It is for your safety.

DR CAREW: No. You can not.

DR CAREW begins to fight.

Get off me.

SAL and JOHN battle with him. He is pulled down and pinned to the ground.

JOHN takes the irons.

DR MAYNARD: Be gentle with him.

SAL: Gentle?

DR MAYNARD: Tender. I wish you to be tender.

JOHN: Stay still sir.

JOHN holds out the hand restraints.

DR CAREW: Is this a ring? You marry me?

JOHN: Stay still.

DR CAREW erupts and throws JOHN off.

DR CAREW: Get off me. Get off. I will not be contained in here. I am not one of these.

DR CAREW weeps again.

Do not do this to me.

ANNABEL rushes forward to comfort him.

I do not want you.

DR CAREW spits at her.

Where is my gin seller?

JOHN: Get the belt.

DR MAYNARD: No. I will not allow him to be restrained.

JOHN: We have to, sir.

DR MAYNARD: No.

PHYLLIS steps forward.

PHYLLIS: He wants me.

DR MAYNARD: Help him to his bed.

PHYLLIS: Sir, sir. Come with me.

PHYLLIS gestures and they all step back.

DR CAREW: I know what they will do.

PHYLLIS: Here.

DR CAREW: I will bleed pints but they will still cut me. I will vomit until my entrails hang out from my mouth. I will shit in buckets and piss in gin bottles.
What have I done?

PHYLLIS: You are ill sir.

DR CAREW stops, looks at PHYLLIS. He stares.

PHYLLIS: What is it?

DR CAREW touches her face.

DR CAREW: Look upon your cheek. A beetle rests.

PHYLLIS brushes her cheek.

PHYLLIS: I have no beetle.

DR CAREW: And here another. Your hair is alive with the wings and the antennae. Look, do you not hear their wings beating?

PHYLLIS: I only hear your breathing.

DR CAREW pushes her away.

DR CAREW: Do not touch me or come near me.
The wings are tangled in your hair and I want for my mother.

PHYLLIS: Now come on, sir. Have a little of this.

PHYLLIS gives him a small bottle.

DR CAREW: I want only to be a child and be in a field with tall grass and only the sky to see.
Your eyes.

DR CAREW pulls back, scared.

PHYLLIS: What?

DR CAREW: They crawl upon you. Your eyes. No. Look away. This house is too noisy.

PHYLLIS: Come, you need somewhere quiet.

DR CAREW: Who are you? I do not know who you are.

PHYLLIS: I have to take you to your bed, sir, then I must go.

DR CAREW: Where must you go? Come with me. Stay here with me.

PHYLLIS: I can't. I'm not mad.

DR CAREW: Stay with me.

PHYLLIS: I have a life to lead, sir.

DR CAREW begins to weep.

Come on, come with me.
That's it. Carefully now.

PHYLLIS leads DR CAREW off, weeping. SAL follows to help. They hand him over.

DR MAYNARD turns to ANNABEL.

DR MAYNARD: Are you all right?

ANNABEL: I think so.

DR MAYNARD hands her his handkerchief and she wipes herself.

DR MAYNARD: Get the lady a drink.

BILLY fetches a drink.

You must go home.

ANNABEL: Yes.

DR MAYNARD: He will be safe here. I will ensure he is looked after.

ANNABEL: I know.

DR MAYNARD: We will get the best help for him.

ANNABEL: Or course.

SAL returns.

DR MAYNARD: Is he quiet?

SAL: He is raving, but he can't come to no harm in there.

DR MAYNARD: Good.

PHYLLIS returns.

ANNABEL: *(To PHYLLIS)* Get out. *(To DR MAYNARD)* Get her out.

JOHN steps forward.

JOHN: My wife, madam, allow me to remove her.

PHYLLIS: Your wife. You're a wet sponge. A pudding.

JOHN: I am no pudding. Madam. Out.

PHYLLIS: No.

JOHN: I will make you.

PHYLLIS: You ain't never made no-one do nothing.

JOHN: Watch.

JOHN picks up PHYLLIS.

PHYLLIS: John.

JOHN: Shut up.

JOHN removes her.

BILLY gives ANNABEL the drink.

ANNABEL: Thank you.
Who are you?

BILLY strips off.

SAL: He ain't no-one. Get out. Go on.

BILLY: I've come for May. She and I were to be married
before they sent me to sea.

ANNABEL: Why are you here?

BILLY: I wanted to get her out. May. Come to me. Come on.

LAURENCE overhears and rushes out.

LAURENCE: Do not believe what he says. I have come for May. Do not, gentlemen, allow this poor woman to go with this uncouth sheep herder. She doesn't want a clod-hopping, udder-yanking, plough-trailing, shit-picking ninnyhammer.

BILLY: Shut up.
This "gentleman" shouldn't be here, sir. He paid money to the woman what guards at night.

DR MAYNARD: But who is he?

GARDENIA enters with STELLA.

GARDENIA: Doctor. Annabel. Laurence. Good morning.

LAURENCE: It is not me.

GARDENIA: It is clearly you.

BILLY: He's come for my May.

LAURENCE: She is my May.

BILLY moves forward.

BILLY: May? I've come to take you home.

MAY: Who is this?

LAURENCE: You see, she has no idea who he is.

DR MAYNARD: Who allowed you in?

BILLY: It was this one. He gave her money and she let him in.

BILLY points out SAL.

DR MAYNARD: You allowed this man in last night?

SAL: No, sir.

DR MAYNARD: Search her.

SAL: I ain't done nothing.

SAL is searched. JOHN finds the money.

ANNABEL holds up the money.

ANNABEL: Then what is this?

SAL: I ain't never seen it before.

ANNABEL: Take her away.

SAL: You can't do that. All my life I been working. Looking
after these lunatics.
I ain't done nothing wrong.

ANNABEL: Get her out.

SAL: You snit catching rat.

SAL is taken off.

GARDENIA: Doctor, would you take this? A letter from a mad
doctor of my acquaintance.

She hands over a paper.

DR MAYNARD: "Laurence Steele has become infatuated with
a young woman who has not been of sound mind. He has
entered a state of high excitement where he is convinced of
unreal events."

LAURENCE: Who is this doctor?

DR MAYNARD: "It is recommended that he be locked up for
the sake of his state of mind, and be placed in a quiet place
until equilibrium has returned."

LAURENCE: Lock me up? This is preposterous.

GARDENIA: It is what the doctor suggests.

LAURENCE: There is nothing wrong with me.

GARDENIA: I think the doctor will listen to another doctor, rather than you.

DR MAYNARD: It is written here.

LAURENCE: She has orchestrated it.

GARDENIA: You said you wanted your name and visage recognised where're you go. You will have it on visiting days.

LAURENCE: You are a bracket-faced grog-blossomed hell cat. Sir, this is a vendetta.

DR MAYNARD: *(Shouts.)* Silence.

The cellar opens and OLIVER emerges blinking, his eyes unused to the light.

As Governor, I shall now regain order.
From today, there will be no alcohol. No music. The doors will be locked and there will be no visitors to gawp and prod.

ANNABEL: Thank God.

DR MAYNARD: Patients will be treated with care and compassion, and it will be understood they need silence and privacy. Glass shall be placed in windows. This is the new Bedlam. Do you all understand?
Good.
These two men *(Gestures at OLIVER and LAURENCE.)* will share a room on this floor.
John?

JOHN: Sir.

DR MAYNARD: Ensure this man has his materials. Here is your subject.

OLIVER circles LAURENCE.

LAURENCE: You can't put me in with him.

OLIVER: You have good bones.

LAURENCE: They are my bones.

OLIVER rubs his hands together.

OLIVER: I can make a pretty picture of him. Does he have a hat?

GARDENIA passes him a hat. OLIVER places it on LAURENCE, adjusts it.

DR MAYNARD: Take them away.

LAURENCE: No.

LAURENCE sinks to his knees. Cries, pleads.

Please, no. I will make it up. I will do anything. Not this. Stella. Have pity on me.

STELLA: Pity? What is pity?

LAURENCE and OLIVER are taken away.

You won't keep him for too long?

DR MAYNARD: Until his mind is quiet.

GARDENIA: Good. Let us go then. We go to dinner this evening, so we need to dress.

STELLA: Thank you, doctor.

DR MAYNARD: My pleasure.

STELLA and GARDENIA leave.

Matthew. Tomorrow we will do admissions together.

MATTHEW: Will you teach me to be a mad doctor?

DR MAYNARD: I will try.

MATTHEW: Thank you. Thank you.

MATTHEW grabs NANCY and dances with joy. They dance off. MAY walks around BILLY.

MAY: This ain't my Billy.

BILLY: I'll prove I am.

DR MAYNARD: She says you're not.

BILLY: She don't know what's going on. I'll prove she knows
me. Watch.
(To MAY.) Where's the sea?

No response.

We're on the clifftop, May. Looking over the sea. Cows is
lying down. Got to be rain coming.

MAY: No.

BILLY: They seen us, they're getting up now. They're going in
for milking. You coming? Let's follow them in. You there
with them? Hup hup. She's lagging, ain't she?

MAY: Yeh.

BILLY: Smack her on the arse, get her going.

MAY: Lazy cow.

BILLY: Stubborn bugger, ain't she?

MAY laughs.

That's it, May.

MAY looks at him. Billy starts to sing.

My one love, my true love, my boy from the sea,
He left me behind and he whispered to me,
"My one love, my sweet love, take a lock of my hair,
One day I'll be back and I'll make us a pair."

MAY: Billy?

MAY runs at BILLY, who holds her. MAY sings the last verse.

My one love, my true love, my boy from the sea,
By bird's wing and fish fin he came back to me,
My one love, my sweet love, he came to the city,
By cow's back and horse hoof he'll make me his pretty.

It is you. You come back for me.

BILLY: It is.

Sir. Doctor, sir. I request that I be allowed to stay with her and take her out into London's fields, sir. That's where she needs to be.

ANNABEL: Why not?

DR MAYNARD: Then I will give my permission.

BILLY: Thank you.

BILLY and MAY leave.

ANNABEL and DR MAYNARD are alone.

ANNABEL coughs.

DR MAYNARD: Are you unwell?

ANNABEL: No. I merely needed to clear my throat.

DR MAYNARD: Ah. I also get a throat which needs clearing.

Clears his throat.

You see.
I am not here for long.

ANNABEL: No?

DR MAYNARD: I will check on the patients and ensure they are cared for, then I am leaving.

ANNABEL: Doctor.

DR MAYNARD: Yes.

ANNABEL: You are a compassionate man.

DR MAYNARD: It is impossible to be with these people and not feel compassion.

ANNABEL: Not everyone shares that view.

DR MAYNARD: I know. All we can do is try to understand. To share knowledge and perhaps one day we will know more.

ANNABEL: I think the more we have, the more opulent our lives, the more we suffer greed and vanity, and the madder we get.

DR MAYNARD: Perhaps one day we'll see that is the case. To me, the human mind is so delicately balanced that it is a miracle any one of us is deemed to be sane.

ANNABEL: Have you ever felt as they do?

DR MAYNARD: A man's passions are close to madness. They only feel what we feel, but magnified.

ANNABEL: You are admirably committed.

DR MAYNARD: I fear so.

ANNABEL: So much that you never married.

DR MAYNARD: I never found the time.

ANNABEL: Nor perhaps the right woman.

DR MAYNARD: Perhaps.

ANNABEL: A man needs a woman. A man without a woman is a bird without wings. A fish without water.

DR MAYNARD: Then I fear I must be drowning.

Looks around.

This would be a pleasant place to while away time, but I must leave. I have other patients, Madam.

ANNABEL: What would happen if you stayed?

DR MAYNARD: My paitents would go without care.

ANNABEL: You still place them before yourself?

DR MAYNARD: Do I?

ANNABEL: You do, yes.

DR MAYNARD: I really do need to go.

ANNABEL: Then leave.

DR MAYNARD: Yes.
Perhaps I am not too busy that I couldn't dawdle.

ANNABEL: Do you like to dawdle?

DR MAYNARD: I am not convinced I ever have. I am trying it out.

Clears his throat again.

Perhaps you would like to come and dawdle with me.

ANNABEL: Yes. Yes.

DR MAYNARD: How would you feel about taking my arm? We have to walk through the unsavoury streets.

ANNABEL: I would love to.

DR MAYNARD: Then you shall.

ANNABEL takes his arm and they leave.

SCENE SIX

MAY and BILLY walk to London Fields. BILLY leads MAY by the hand.

MAY: Where are we? You said we were to go the fields.

BILLY: These are the fields.

MAY: There's no real grass. There's no animals.

BILLY: But look there's stuff growing. There's vegetables and crops.

MAY: Can you see the birds? Look.

MAY points up.

BILLY: May. Come here.

BILLY tries to hold her. MAY pulls away and watches the birds.

MAY: I'm watching them.

BILLY: I want to take you home.
We'll go back and you can come and live with me.

MAY: Where will we live?

BILLY: I don't know. Your father won't have us anywhere near. We'll have to get our own piece of land. I'll plant some fruit trees and we'll stand underneath them each autumn and catch the fruits.
We will be all right. Oh, May. I knew what made you ill was me going away.

MAY: Have I been ill?

BILLY: Yeh. But I'm going to look after you.
Look, May, see the big dome.

MAY: There.

BILLY: There, yeh. And all the houses. The city of London. I'll get you out of here. We'll go back to the real fields, find a house for the two of us.

MAY: Will we have a house?

BILLY: We'll have a house with a roof and windows and we'll get ourselves some cows and a dog.

MAY: And some hens.

BILLY: And you'll collect the eggs.
May. Come here.

BILLY holds her.

You give us a kiss.

They kiss.

May, you will marry me, won't you?

They kiss again and, as they kiss, the stage is instantly transformed into a wedding with all the guests. The NARRATOR is the vicar.

NARRATOR: Dearly Beloved, we are gathered here today to join this man and this woman in holy matrimony.
I require and charge you both that if either of you know any impediment why you may not be lawfully joined together, confess now or ever hold your piece.

MAY: Stop.

BILLY: What is it?

NARRATOR: Speak now, or hold your peace.

MAY: Shhh. The birds.

NARRATOR: What birds?

MAY: I can hear everything. Their wing feathers brush against each other.
They're talking to each other. No. They're talking to me.

MAY listens, laughs.

You hear them?

BILLY: No. May? We have to do this.

MAY: Wait. They're asking me something. *(To birds.)* What? I don't know. I said I don't know. Oh, all right. I'll ask him. *(To BILLY.)* The birds want me to ask you. Can they have that shiny ring you're holding?

BILLY: May, it's your wedding ring.

MAY: Oh. *(To birds.)* You hear that? *(Listens.)* I don't know. I'll ask him. *(To BILLY.)* What is a wedding ring?

BILLY: May, shut up and get on with it.

BILLY slips the ring onto MAY's hand and kisses her again.

BILLY stands back and they walk through an arch of guests who hold boughs of May Blossom.

MUSIC

ACT ONE:

1. *Boys of Bedlam.* Traditional.

2. *Bedlam.* Folk Songs from Somerset, Cecil Sharp, 1905.

3. *Four Drunken Nights.* The Child Ballads, adapted and updated.

ACT TWO:

4. *Oyster Nan.* Thomas Durfey's Pills to Purge Melancholy, 1719.

5. *Loving Mad Tom.* Old Ballads, Thomas Evans, 1810.

6. *Sea Shanty.* Words by the author.